Robertson's British Tax-tables, on an Improved Plan; Containing all the Taxes Which Affect Every Description of men, Both in England and Scotland.

ROBERTSON's
BRITISH
TAX-TABLES,

ON AN IMPROVED PLAN,

CONTAINING

All the TAXES *which affect every deſcription of Men,*

BOTH IN ENGLAND AND SCOTLAND

Together with

USEFUL REGULATIONS FOR THE CITIES OF
LONDON AND EDINBURGH

LONDON.

Printed for and Sold by all the Bookſellers.

MDCCXCII

PREFACE

THE multiplicity of laws now in exiſtence for raiſing the public revenue, renders it impoſſible, for any perſon to retain in his memory, the various taxes incident to almoſt every ſituation of life To obviate this difficulty, many uſeful abridgements have been ſucceſsfully publiſhed, under the name of Tax Tables, and although much merit is due to the compilers for the general utility of their labours, there yet ſeems room for ſome improvement to be made, at leaſt as far as relates to this country For this purpoſe, the following conciſe Tables are offered to the public In theſe they will find all the material acts that apply to both countries, many uſeful tables added, which never has appeared in any book of the kind, and abſtracts of the particular

Excise laws and regulations for the Scottish distilleries, to which are added, the temporary regulations for coaches, chairs, carts, porters, &c in the city of Edinburgh and Leith

As this is the first publication of Tax Tables ever attempted in this kingdom, it has been the study of the publisher to make them generally useful to every station, and as much labour and expence has been bestowed on the compilation, he hopes the encouragement of a generous public will enable him to fulfil his intentions of continuing them with such alterations as may be made from time to time by the legislature

ROBERTSON's

BRITISH

TAX-TABLES.

ASSESSED TAXES.

DUTIES ON HORSES, COACHES, WAGGONS, WAINS, AND CARTS.

I. *Coaches and other Carriages, (except Waggons, Wains, and Carts.)*

BY the Act 25 Geo. III. c. 47, called the *Transfer Act*, there shall be paid

For every coach, berlin, landau, chariot, calash with four wheels, chaise marine, chaise with four wheels, and caravan, or by whatever name such carriages may be called, kept by any person for his own use, or to be let out to hire, (except Hackney coaches) the yearly sum of 7l. and by the 29th Geo. III. c. 49. 20s. more: in the whole 8l. for the first carriage, 9l. for the second, by 29th Geo. III. c. 43. and where three or more carriages are kept, 8l. for the first, and 10l. for each after the first.

And for every calash, chaise, chair, gig, or whiskey, or by whatever name they are known or called, having two or three wheels, to be drawn by one or more horses, that shall be kept by any person for his own use, or to be let out to hire, the yearly sum of 3l. 10s. 29th Geo. III. c. 49.

The duties on coaches, waggons, wains, and carts, and on riding horses, shall be assessed, collected, and received by such persons, and in like manner, as the duties on houſes and windows, namely, by the Commiſſioners of Taxes, who are to put this act in execution, 25 Geo. III c. 47

If aſſeſſors neglect their duty, ſurveyors and inſpectors may perform the ſame. Aſſeſſors not to act on pain of 20l before they take an oath to charge all perſons *according to the beſt of their judgment and knowledge*. Commiſſioners to give notice in their precepts that the aſſeſſors of the duties on houſes and windows, are alſo aſſeſſors of the duties upon carriages, horſes, and ſervants.

Aſſeſſors to give notice in writing to perſons keeping carriages or horſes or ſervants, to produce in fourteen days after ſuch notice, liſts of the number kept by them, and in caſe ſuch liſts are not delivered, the aſſeſſor ſhall, from the beſt information he can obtain, make an aſſeſſment on ſuch perſons ſo refuſing, which ſhall be final and concluſive, unleſs the perſon aſſeſſed ſhall make a ſufficient excuſe before the Commiſſioners. Theſe liſts muſt contain the greater number kept between the 5th of July, 1784, and the 5th of April, 1785.

Commiſſioners, on application, may grant relief to perſons who have been aſſeſſed in different places for the ſame carriages or horſes.

In caſe the liſts delivered to the aſſeſſors ſhall be deficient, they may ſurcharge the ſame, and they are to deliver their aſſeſſments to the commiſſioners within three months after their appointment, and the commiſſioners are to ſign the ſame, and appoint collectors.

Surveyors may inſpect the liſts before they are ſigned, and amend them, and if they diſcover any omiſſions after the liſts are ſigned, they are to certify the ſame to the commiſſioners.

Perſons neglecting to deliver liſts to the aſſeſſor, ſhall forfeit 10l.

Perſons to be doubly rated for thoſe carriages and horſes omitted in their liſts, one half of which ſurcharge ſhall be allowed the aſſeſſor or ſurveyor for making the ſame.

Inhabitant houſeholders ſhall deliver liſts of lodg-

ers who keep carriages or horses, containing the names of such lodgers, on the penalty of 10l

Persons over rated may appeal to the commissioners, and the appellant shall deliver on oath a list of the greatest number of carriages and horses, kept by him

Commissioners shall not make any abatement in the charge or surcharge, unless it shall appear upon oath that the appellant is over rated. Ten days notice to be given of appeal Commissioners in certain cases, may remit the penalty before directed to be paid to the assessor, surveyor, or inspector, surcharging such lists.

Surveyor, assessor, or inspector making a false surcharge, shall forfeit such penalties as are directed to be inflicted by the acts relative to the duties on houses and windows, for neglect of duty

Determination of commissioners to be final, but persons dissatisfied therewith may appeal to any Justice of the Courts of King's Bench or Common Pleas, or to one of the Barons of the Exchequer, and in Scotland to the Court of Session or Exchequer, and every such Judge is required, with all convenient speed to return an answer to such case with his opinion thereon subscribed thereto, according to which opinion, the assessment which shall have been the cause of such appeal shall be altered or confirmed.

Penalties exceeding 20l shall be recovered in any court of record at Westminster, or in the courts of Scotland, one moiety thereof to the king, and the other to the informer

Penalties not exceeding 20l may be recovered before two Justices, and may be levied by distress.

All actions or informations shall be brought within one year after the offence committed, and defendant may plead the general issue and recover treble costs.

The 29th Geo. III c. [illegible], after specifying that several carriages are used for pleasure and are entered and paid for as carts or carriages, liable to smaller duties, and that the name of the proprietor is put thereon, in order to evade the payment of the higher duties as specified by the 29th of Geo. III enacts that every carriage that hath two or three wheels, by whatever name they are now or hereafter may be called, drawn by one or more horses, which shall be used at any time for the carriage or conveyance of persons, and not generally in the affairs of husbandry, merchandize, or for the carriage of goods, &c. shall be deemed a carriage within the meaning of the act of the 25th Geo. III. and paid for accordingly, under a penalty of 7l. for every carriage so used. 29th Geo. III. c. 49.

II. *Horses.*

BY 24 Geo. III. c. 31. and 25 Geo. III. c. 47. every person who shall keep and use any horse for the purpose of riding, or of drawing any coach, berlin, chariot, chaise, or other carriage, in respect whereof any duty is payable, shall pay annually for every such horse 10s. And by 29 Geo. III. c. 49, 5s. more for one of such horses, *in the whole* 15s.

Where three, four, or five are kept, an additional 7s. 6d. for each above the first, 29 Geo. III. c. 49, *in the whole*, 17s. 6d. for each above the first.

And where six or more are kept, an additional 10s. for each above the first, 29 Geo. III. c. 49, in the whole 1l. for each above the first.

By 24 Geo. III. c. 31. and 29 Geo. III. c. 49, it is provided that nothing therein shall charge any horse belonging to any non-commissioned officer, or private soldier, of any regiment of cavalry in the king's service, nor any horse belonging to, and kept for sale and not for hire, in the stable of a licensed dealer, not let to hire for travelling post by the mile, or from stage to stage, or let to hire for a day or less period of time, by any postmaster, innkeeper, or person licensed by the Commissioners of stamp duties.

The duties of the 24th and of the 29th, are to be paid by all persons using or hiring horses or carriages by the year, month, or any other period, not the person who lets them out. 29 Geo. III. c. 49.

The additional duties are not to extend to carriages let out to travel post by any person licensed to let post horses. 29 Geo. III. c. 49. *Such carriages, therefore, pay* only 7l.

Horse dealers are to give in a list of such as they keep for riding or drawing, and pay the duty. 29th Geo. III. c. 49.

No person keeping a horse, &c. used really for husbandry, or drawing any carriage, (except such as was heretofore liable to an Excise duty) or carrying burdens in the course of the trade of the person to whom such horse, &c. shall belong, shall be chargeable with the duty, in case such horse, &c. shall not be used for any other purpose of riding, except *when returning from any place to which any load or burden shall by such horse, &c. have been carried, or going to any place from whence a burden is to be carried, or being rid to procure medical assistance, or to or from market, or place of public worship, or election of members to serve in parliament, or to or from any court of justice, or to or from any meeting of commissioners of taxes.* 26th Geo. III. c. 70.

A horse, &c. where the owners are through poverty excused the usual taxes of church and poor, are also exempted.

No person occupying a farm less than 70l. a year, and making a livelihood solely thereby, shall be chargeable with the duty for any horse occasionally used in riding, if such horse be *bona fide* kept for the purpose of husbandry.

III. *Waggons, Wains, Carts, &c.*

BY the 23d Geo. III. c. 66, every person who shall keep any waggon, wain, cart, or other such carriage, with three or four wheels (except such as are already charged with a duty under the management of the Commissioners of Excise) shall pay annually 4s. for each; if with two wheels, 2s. for each.

Provided that no person shall be obliged to pay the said yearly sum of 4s. for more than one such carriage employed in agriculture only, nor for more than three such carriages employed for any other purpose, if kept by him for his own use only, and not used for the carriage of goods for hire, or to be let out for hire.

Provided also, that no person shall be obliged to pay the said yearly sum of 2s. for any cart or other carriage with two wheels, employed in agriculture only, and not employed in parks or pleasure grounds, or used for the carriage of goods for hire, or let out for hire, or if drawn by one horse only, and employed only for the carriage of peats or turf for fuel, and not let out for hire.

And provided that if any waggon or other carriage shall be pressed for conveying any arms, ammunition, or other baggage, under the acts against mutiny and desertion, or for the regulation of the King's marine forces whilst on shore, and the owners shall be paid for the same, this shall not be deemed a working for hire.

The management of these duties is by 25 Geo. III c. 47, placed under the Commissioners of Taxes.

PERFUMERY

(26 Geo. III. c. 49.)

FROM and after the 5th of July 1786, the following new duties are to be paid throughout Great Britain.

Upon every packet, box, bottle, phial, or other inclosure, containing any powders, pastes, balls, waters, washes, or other composition whatsoever, commonly called sweet scents, odours, perfumes, cosmeticks, &c. to be used as sweet scents, odours, perfumes, or cosmeticks, which shall be vended in Great Britain, mixed or unmixed with other materials, there shall be charged a stamp duty as hereafter expressed; and also upon every packet, &c. containing any dentrifice, or other preparation for the teeth or gums, which shall be vended in Great Britain, there shall be charged a stamp duty as hereafter expressed, and upon every roll, cake, or piece, packet, box, &c. containing any preparation for the hair, which shall be vended in Great Britain, there shall be charged a stamp duty, as hereafter expressed, and also upon every packet containing any hair powder, which shall be vended in Great Britain, the price whereof shall exceed two shillings for the pound weight, there shall be charged a stamp duty according to the like rates hereafter expressed, that is to say, For every packet of perfume under eight pence value, a duty of [illegible]

Between eight pence and one shilling 1d. halfpenny.

Between one shilling and two shillings and sixpence [illegible]

Between two shillings and sixpence and five shillings 6d.

Five shillings and upwards 1s.

For every packet of hair powder, not exceeding two shillings per lb. 1d. duty upon every pound weight, or any less quantity.

This act is not to extend to drugs, pills, waters, essences, &c. which are charged with rates or duties by an act of the 23d of Geo. III. c. 79, nor to common soap unmixed with perfumes.

Persons who sell all or any of the articles hereby taxed are to take out an annual licence for which they shall pay one Shilling.

These duties to be under the management of the Commissioners of the Stamp Office, who shall grant licences to all that apply for them.

Every person vending the above goods after the 5th of July 1786 without a licence, forfeits 5l.

All venders of the above goods not having after the said 5th of July the words, "*Licenced to Deal in Perfumery*," on the front of their houses, or over their doors, written in large characters, within 20 days after their licence has been granted, forfeits 5l.

Unlicenced persons fixing such notice on their houses forfeit 20l.

Venders must send for the wrappers, covers, or labels of their bottles and parcels to the commissioners as they shall direct, and pay for them on delivery.

Every person selling a packet, &c. without the stamp forfeits 5l.

Hair powder, not exceeding two shillings per lb. in value, may be sold wholesale by the maker, not less than 224 lb. to any person licenced by this act, free of duty, ſuch maker having made a true entry of it at any Exciſe Office, as is required by ſeveral ſtatutes.

Such makers and wholeſale venders muſt keep a book for the inſpection of the proper officer, containing the quantities, dates of ſale, and names of the perſons to whom each parcel was ſold, on forfeit 20l.

Any perſon uſing a ſtamp twice forfeits 50l.

Perſons buying, ſelling, or bartering ſtamps or marks to be uſed a ſecond time, or buying or ſelling packets with ſuch labels, forfeit 10l.

Five per cent. diſcount is allowed on the ſtamps upon preſent payment.

N. B. The [illegible] *ſtamp is to be allowed* [illegible] *mentioned.*

Before a licence is obtained, notice ſhall be ſent in writing to the Commiſſioners of the Stamp Office, of the place of vending wares or articles liable to theſe duties, and alſo when the place of vending is changed, or in default forfeit 5l.

And all ſuch wares, and other articles, ſubject to the duties hereby impoſed, which ſhall be kept ready or offered for ſale in any ſhop or other place whereof notice ſhall have been given as aforeſaid (except *Almond Paſte,* [illegible] *Powder, Bear's Greaſe, Cold Cream,* [illegible] *hard Soap,* [illegible] *Soap, perfumed and Coloured Hair Powder* [illegible] *2s. per lb. Rouge* [illegible]*, and Waſhballs of all ſorts*, and which ſhall be allowed to be kept and expoſed to ſale in any ſhop or other place, in bulk or otherwiſe, without any ſtamped cover, wrapper, or label affixed thereto until the time of actual ſale thereof) ſhall be deemed to require a cover, wrapper or label marked as by this act is required to be previouſly affixed thereon, in manner to be directed by the ſaid Commiſſioners as aforeſaid.

Proper officers may ſearch ſhops, &c. and where ſtamped covers are wanting, affix the ſame, which muſt be paid for on a penalty of 5l.

Perſons obſtructing officers in the execution of their duty forfeit 20l.

Damaged ſtamps, labels, covers, &c. may be returned for others (upon oath that they have not been uſed) without any expence.

Perſons ſelling articles ſubject to duty in any place not ſpecified, forfeit 5l.

Articles ſold for exportation not to be ſubject to theſe duties.

An account of articles exported to be ſent to the Commiſſioners of the Stamp Office, who will grant certificates to the venders.

Perſons convicted of offences againſt this act forfeit their licence, and cannot have another without giving a bond for 100l. and upon conviction of a ſecond offence 50l. which will be ſued for when forfeited.

Counterfeiting the ſtamp is a capital offence.

Informers are intitled to half if ſued for within ſix months, but not after.

Juſtices may determine matters relative to pecuniary penalties, and mitigate half if they think proper.

GAME LICENCES

(25 Geo. III. c. 50. and 31 Geo. III. c. 21.)

FROM July 1, 1785, there ſhall be paid to his Majeſty the following duties:

Every perſon in Great Britain, who ſhall uſe any dog, gun, net, or other engine for the taking or deſtruction of game (not acting as gamekeeper) ſhall deliver in a paper or account in writing, containing his name and place of abode, to the clerk of the peace or his deputy, and annually take out a certificate thereof, and every ſuch certificate ſhall be charged with a ſtamp-duty of 2l. 2s. and an addition of 1l. 1s. by 31 Geo. III. c. 21, making in the whole 3l. 3s.

Every deputation of a gamekeeper ſhall be regiſtered with the clerk of the peace, and ſuch gamekeeper ſhall annually take out a certificate thereof, which certificate ſhall be charged with a ſtamp duty of 10s. 6d. and an additional 10s. 6d. by 31 Geo. III. c. 21, making in the whole 1l. 1s.

The duties to be under the management of the commiſſioners of the ſtamp office.

From and after the [illegible] of July [illegible] the clerk of the peace fhall annually deliver to the perfons refpectively requiring the fame, duly ftamped, a certificate or licence according to the form thereto annexed, for which he fhall be entitled to demand 1s. for his trouble; and on refufal or neglect to deliver the fame forfeit [illegible]

Every certificate to bear date the day when iffued, and to continue in force until the 1ft day of July then following, on penalty of [illegible]

After the [illegible] day of July [illegible], any perfon that fhall ufe any greyhound, hound, pointer, fetting-dog, fpaniel, or other dog, or any gun, net, or engine for taking or killing of game, without a certificate, is liable to the penalty of [illegible]

From the faid 1ft day of July [illegible] that any game-keeper fhall, for the fpace of twenty days after the faid 1ft day of July, or if any gamekeeper thereafter to be appointed fhall, for the fpace of twenty days next after fuch appointment [illegible] or refufe to regifter his deputation and take out a certificate thereof, he is liable to the penalty of [illegible]

This act not to extend to the royal family.

The clerks of the peace are to tranfmit to the ftamp-office in London, alphabetical lifts of the certificates granted, every year before the 1ft day of Auguft, under penalty of 20l

The lift to be kept at the ftamp-office in London, and there to be infpected on payment of 1s.

The commiffioners of the ftamp-duties are once or oftener in every year, as foon as fuch lifts are tranfmitted to them, to caufe the fame to be publifhed in the newfpapers [illegible] each county, or fuch public papers as they fhall think moft proper.

If any gamekeeper who fhall have regiftered his deputation and take out a certificate thereof, fhall be changed, and a new gamekeeper appointed in his ftead, the firft certificate is declared null and void, and the perfon [illegible] under the fame after notice, is liable to the penalty of [illegible]

Any perfon in purfuit of game who fhall refufe to produce his certificate, or to tell his name and place of abode, or shall give in any false or fictitious name or place of abode to any person requiring the same, who shall have obtained a certificate, is liable to the penalty of 50l.

The certificates are not to authorize persons to kill game at any time prohibited by law, nor to give any person any right to kill game, unless such person shall be qualified so to do by the laws now in being; but shall be liable to the same penalties as if this act had not passed.

(So that though by this act qualified and unqualified persons are equally included, yet having a certificate does not give an unqualified person a right to kill game; the point of RIGHT still stands upon the former acts of parliament; and any unqualified person killing game without a certificate, is not only liable to the penalty inflicted by this act, but also to all the former penalties relating to the killing of game, &c.) Witnesses refusing to appear on Justices summons, or appearing and refusing to give evidence, forfeit 10l.

The certificates obtained under deputations not to be given in evidence for killing of game by a gamekeeper out of the manor, in respect of which such deputation or appointment was given and made.

Persons counterfeiting stamps, to suffer death as felons.

Penalties exceeding 20l. are to be recovered in any of his Majesty's Courts of Record at Westminster; and penalties not exceeding 20l. are recoverable before two justices, and may be levied by distress.

N. B. The whole of the above penalties go to the informer.

GAME LAWS.

A Short Sketch of the LAWS, as they now stand, relating to Hares, Partridges, Pheasants, and other Game.

THE penalty for killing in the night a hare, partridge, or pheasant, qualified or unqualified, is 5l.

Any unqualified person exposing to sale a hare, partridge, pheasant, or other game, is liable to a penalty of 5l.

If any hare, pheasant, partridge, or other game, be found in the shop, house, or possession of any poulterer, salesman, fishmonger, cook, or pastry-cook, or of any person not qualified in his own right to kill game, or entitled thereunto under some person so qualified, it shall be deemed an exposing thereof to sale.

For selling a hare, partridge, pheasant, or other game, qualified or unqualified, 5l.

Any unqualified person using tunnels or other engines, to kill or destroy a hare, partridge, pheasant, or other game, forfeits 5l.

Any unqualified person keeping and using greyhounds, setting-dogs, lurchers, tunnels, or other engines, to kill or destroy hares, partridges, pheasants, or other game, is liable to 5l. penalty. The 5l. penalty is not for keeping without using.

For killing a partridge between the 12th of February and 1st of September, qualified or unqualified, 5l.

For killing a pheasant, between the 1st of February and 1st of October, qualified or unqualified, 5l.

For using greyhounds, lurchers, or setting-dogs*, to kill a hare, partridge, or pheasant, unqualified, 5l.

(The information in the above cases must be laid within six calendar months, before a justice of the peace, or by action of debt, bill, plaint, or information. The whole penalty to be given to the informer, with double costs, if brought on in the courts of Westminster.) Half to informer and half to poor.

For tracing in the snow, or shooting with a gun or long bow, a hare, qualified or unqualified, imprisonment three months, or fine 1l.

For using snares to take or kill a hare, qualified or unqualified, imprisonment one month, or fine 10s.

* *Greyhounds, lurchers, and setting-dogs, are the only dogs for keeping and using which the penalty of 5l. is levied. But by another statute, a penalty not exceeding 20s. may be levied for keeping and using the above or any other dogs.*

(The information in the above cases must be laid before a justice of the peace within one year.)

The informer to be entitled to half costs and charges, and to half the penalty, the other half to be given to the poor of the parish.

Any game keeper killing or taking a hare, pheasant, partridge, or other game, under colour of keeping for the use of the lord of the manor, and afterwards selling and disposing thereof without the consent of the said lord of the manor, upon conviction, on the complaint of such lord, upon the oath of one witness, before a justice, shall be committed to the house of correction for three months, and there kept to hard labour.

Any person who shall destroy, sell, or buy any hare, pheasant, &c. and shall in three months make discovery of any higgler, chapman, carrier, innkeeper, alehouse keeper, or victualler, that hath bought or sold, or offered to buy or sell, or had in their possession, any hare, pheasant, partridge, &c. so as any one shall be convicted, such discoverer shall be discharged of the pains and penalties hereby enacted for killing or selling such game, and shall receive the same benefit as any other informer.

Any justice of the peace, and lord of a manor within his manor, may take away any such hare, pheasant, partridge, &c. from any higgler, chapman, innkeeper, victualler, or carrier, or any other person not qualified, which shall be found in his custody or possession.

Any person that shall knowingly and wilfully kill, take, or destroy, or use any gun, dog, snare, net, or other engine, with intent to kill, take, or destroy, any hare, partridge, or other game, in the night, viz. between the hours of seven at night and six in the morning, from the 12th of October to the 12th of February, and between the hours of nine at night and four in the morning, from the 12th of February to the 12th of October, or in the day-time on a Sunday or Christmas day, shall forfeit for the first offence not exceeding 20l. nor less than 10l. For the second offence not exceeding 30l. nor less than 20l. For the third and every other subsequent offence 50l.

(The information to be laid within one calendar month, before a justice of the peace. The informer to be intitled to all cofts and charges, and to half the penalty, the other half to be given to the poor of the parifh.)

No perfon fhall fhoot with any crofs bow, hand-gun, or demihake, unlefs fuch perfon is really poffeffed of 100l. per annum, on pain of forfeiting 10l.

No perfon of what eftate or degree foever, fhall fhoot with, carry, keep, ufe, or have in his poffeffion, any hand-gun, not being in the ftock and gun of the length of one yard, or any hagbut, or demihake, not being in the ftock and gun of the length of three quarters of a yard, on pain of forfeiting 10l.

Any perfon having 100l. per annum as above, may feize every fuch crofs-bow, hand-gun, &c. being fo deficient in length, but fhall break and deftroy them in twenty days after fuch feizure, on pain of forfeiting 2l.

No perfon fhall command his fervant to fhoot with any crofs-bow, hand-gun, hagbut, or demihake, at any deer, fowl, or other thing, except at a butt or bank of earth, on pain of forfeiting 10l.

N. B. Perfons qualified to kill game, muft be in poffeffion of lands, tenements, or fome other eftate of inheritance, either in right of themfelves or their wives, for life, of the clear yearly value of 100l. or a leafe or leafes of 99 years of 150l. per annum, other than the fon and heir of an efquire, or perfon of a higher degree, or lord of a manor, or keepers of parks, chafes, free warrens, &c.

LORD MANSFIELD's OPINION

An unqualified perfon may go out to beat the hedges, bufhes, &c. with a qualified perfon, and to fee the game purfued or deftroyed; provided the unqualified perfon has no gun or other engine with him for the deftruction of the game, without being fubject to a penalty.

GLO[illegible]ES.

(2[illegible] Geo III c [illegible])

FROM and after the [illegible] of August, 1[illegible]5, [illegible] persons [illegible] Britain vending gloves or mittens by retail, made of silk, leather, linen, or any other material or [illegible] must take out a licence annually, for which they must pay ONE SHILLING.

For every pair of gloves or mittens let them be made of what they will above the price of four pence, [illegible] exceeding ten pence, [illegible] penny [illegible]

All above ten pence, and not exceeding one shilling and four pence, a duty of [illegible]

All above one shilling and four pence, a duty of 3d.

These duties are to be paid at the Stamp Office, where the venders of gloves [illegible] receive paper tickets, or stamps to be affixed to the gloves, upon application, or of their agents in the country.

Persons selling gloves or mittens without a licence, after the [illegible] of [illegible], [illegible] forfeit for every offence 20l.

These licences to be renewed annually, ten days before the expiration of the former.

Persons vending gloves and mittens must have the words "Dealer in Gloves" painted conspicuously over their shop door or [illegible] where such goods are sold, or forfeit [illegible] for every [illegible] so sold.

Any person who writes or causes to be written, such words, viz. "Dealer in Gloves," without taking out a licence, shall forfeit [illegible]

Any person selling less than twelve dozen pair of gloves or mittens to one person at one time, shall be deemed a retailer.

The tickets expressing the respective duties, to be placed as the commissioners or their agents shall direct upon the inside of the right-hand glove of each pair.

[illegible] gloves or mittens without stamps, or [illegible] of less value than this [illegible] shall forfeit [illegible] licence [illegible]

Licenced dealers may sell to each other without the stamps.

Removing the stamp from one pair of gloves which have been sold to another pair which have not been sold, with a fraudulent intent, or using the same stamp twice, shall forfeit 20l.

Buying or selling any ticket or tickets that have been so fraudulently used is 20l. penalty. Buyer or seller may inform against each other, and the informer will always be indemnified.

Sellers are in their bills of parcels to charge the duty on the stamp, or ticket separate.

Counterfeiting the stamp or mark on the tickets is death, [illegible].

One moiety of every pecuniary penalty goes to the informer, if sued for within the space of six months and not else, beyond that time the whole goes to the King.

Any neighbouring Justice may determine pecuniary penalties, and compel payment, or commit the offender for three months, unless the money is paid sooner.

The Magistrate has power, if he thinks fit, to mitigate one half of the penalty.

The act concludes with a recital of an act still in force, of the 5th of Geo. III. c. 19, relative to and restricting the importation and sale of foreign gloves and mitts; and the 25 Geo. III. also restrains the importation of foreign leather, not completely made into gloves and mitts, but cut into the form of them, and called Shapes or Tranks.

HATS.

Duty on Hats, commenced October 2, 1784.

(24 Geo. III. c. 51.)

LICENCE to sell hats by retail in London, Westminster, Borough, and within the Bills of Mortality - - £2 0 0

Licence in any other part of the kingdom, - 0 5 0

Ditto on every hat of 4s or under	-	£ 0 0 3
Ditto above 4s and not exceeding 7s		0 0 [illegible]
Ditto above 7s and not exceeding 12s		0 1 0
Ditto above 12s and upwards,	- -	0 2 0
No hats sold without licence under forfeiture of	-	50 0 0
"Dealer in Hats" to be written over the door under forfeiture of		[illegible] 0 0
Stamp Tickets affixed to each hat and the crown thereof	- - -	10 0 0
Persons forging the same, or selling hats without tickets affixed, or selling again any tickets, [illegible]		[illegible] 0 0

Office for taking out licences and stamps, Somerset-House

Country Dealers must apply to the Distributers of Stamps in the different counties

---

THEATRICAL REPRESENTATIONS

(28 Geo III c. 30)

BY this act, justices of any county, riding, or liberty in general or quarter sessions assembled, at their discretion, may grant licences to any person or persons applying by petition for the performance of such tragedies, comedies, interludes, operas, plays or farces as now are, or hereafter shall be represented at either of the patent or licensed theatres in the city of Westminster, or as shall in the manner prescribed by law, have been submitted to the inspection of the Lord Chamberlain at any place within their jurisdiction, for any number of days not exceeding sixty, to commence within the then next six months, and to be within the space of such four months as shall be specified in the said licence, so as there be but one licence in use at the same time within the jurisdiction so given, the places so licenced not to be within twenty miles of London, Westminster, or Edinburgh, or eight miles of any patent or licenced theatre, or ten miles of the residence of his Majesty, or any place within the ſame juriſdiction, in which within ſix months preceding, a licence under this act ſhall have been had and exerciſed, or within fourteen miles of either of the univerſities, or within two miles of the outward limits of any city, town or place, having peculiar juriſdiction.

Licences are not to be granted within any place having peculiar juriſdiction, without the conſent of the majority of the juſtices acting for ſuch juriſdiction; neither are licences to be granted unleſs three weeks notice be given to the mayor, bailiff or chief officer previous to their making ſuch application.

REGULATIONS

Of Stage Coach Outſide Paſſengers, Drivers, and Guards.

(30 Geo. III. c. 36.)

THIS act is to alter, explain, and amend the former one of the 28th of Geo. III. c. 57, here they are both conſolidated.

From September 30, 1790, if the driver of any coach, chaiſe, or other carriage of the like ſort, drawn by three or more horſes, travelling for hire, ſhall admit more than one on the coach box beſides himſelf, and four on the roof; or if ſuch carriage be drawn by leſs than three horſes, more than one perſon on the box, and three on the roof, (except the driver of ſuch coach or carriage, drawn by leſs than three horſes, which ſhall not travel a greater diſtance than twenty-five miles from the Poſt-office in the city of London, and who ſhall not carry more than one perſon on the coach box, and four perſons on the roof, at one and the ſame time) to go or be conveyed by any ſuch coach or carriage reſpectively, every ſuch driver ſhall pay the collector of the tolls, at every turnpike through which he paſſes, the ſum of five ſhillings for every perſon above the number ſo as above limited, and every turnpike collector is authoriſed to demand the ſame, every driver attempting to evade the payment of these penalties by setting down or taking up passengers, shall, on being convicted before a justice, be imprisoned in the next goal to where the offence was committed, not more than one month, nor less than fourteen days.

The penalties of five shillings must be recovered in the same manner that the turnpike tolls are.

The name of the proprietor to be painted on each door, except mail coaches. If there are more proprietors than one, and if one of them reside in London or within the bills of mortality, the name of such proprietor shall be the one put upon such carriage.

If the coachman or driver of such coaches or carriages shall permit any other person to drive without the consent of the passengers within such coach, or shall quit the box without reasonable occasion, or longer than such occasion may require, or shall by furiously driving, or by any act of negligence or misconduct overturn the carriage, or in any wise endanger the persons or property of the passengers or owners of the carriage, the coachman or driver so offending shall for every such offence forfeit not more than five pounds, nor less than forty shillings.

If any person acting as a guard to any such carriage shall fire off his arms while the coach is going on the road, or going through or standing in any town, otherwise than for defence of such coach, he shall for every such offence forfeit twenty shillings.

Constables or peace officers refusing to execute warrants, granted by justices pursuant to the directions of this act, shall pay forty shillings, or be committed to prison for a month.

Half the penalties go to the informer, the other half to the surveyors of the highways.

If the driver or offender neglects to obey the justice's summons, or cannot be found, the owner of the carriage must answer.

POST-HORSES

(25 Geo. III. c. 51.)

POSTMASTER, Innkeeper, or person who shall let to hire any horse for travelling post by the mile, or from stage to stage, or being a person usually letting horses to hire, or who shall let to hire for a day or less time, any horse for drawing coach or other carriage used in travelling post, or otherwise, shall pay annually 5s. for a licence.

Persons letting post-horses without a licence, forfeit [illegible] and keeping more than one inn under one licence, 20l.

They are to paint *Licensed to Let Post-Horses* on the front of their houses, on pain of [illegible] l.

For a horse hired by the mile or stage, to be used in travelling post, there shall be charged a duty of *one penny halfpenny* for every mile such horse shall be hired to travel post.

For a horse hired for a day or less time, for drawing on any public road any coach or other carriage used in travelling post, or otherwise, there shall be charged, if the distance shall be then ascertained, one penny halfpenny per mile; and if the distance shall not then be ascertained, 1s. [illegible] for each horse so hired, to be paid by the person by whom the horse shall be hired.

Persons keeping any coach, berlin, landau, chariot, [illegible] chaise, [illegible] chaise, calash, or other carriage, with four wheels, or any calash, chaise, chair, or other carriage with two wheels, to be employed as public stage coaches or carriages, for the purpose of conveying passengers for hire to and from different places, shall pay annually 5s. for a licence.

Every coach, &c. as above, with four wheels, or any chaise, &c. with two wheels, to be employed as aforesaid, shall be charged with a duty of 1d. for every mile such carriage shall travel, to be paid by the owner.

Every person licenced, if they furnish their own chaises or carriages and horses let to hire to travel post, to mark or paint, on the outside pannel of each door of the chaise or carriage, christian and surname, and place of abode, in large and legible characters, in letters of a colour distinct from that of the carriage, each letter at least one inch in length, and continue the same thereupon, as long as such chaise or carriage shall be so used. Neglect or omission, or painting false name or place, incurs a forfeiture of 5l.

Every postmaster, &c. if he furnishes his own coaches, berlins, landaus, chariots, calashes, chaises, or carriages with four wheels, or any calash, chaise, chair, or carriage with two wheels, with horses let to hire for a day, or less, for drawing on any public road, where the carriage shall have a box, or outside seat for driver, shall affix upon some conspicuous part of the foot-board, or other part of the box or seat, a brass or tin plate, on which there shall be marked or engraved christian and surname of owner, and name and place of abode, in large and legible characters, and continue the same thereon, and replace the same as occasion shall require, during the time the coach or carriage shall be so furnished: if no box or outside seat, shall affix upon a conspicuous part of the pole, shaft, or splinter bar of carriage such brass or tin plate, with such engraving thereon, and same to be continued and replaced, or subject to a penalty of 5l. for each default.

Tickets shall be valued in account, and paid for in case of any deficiencies, at the rate of 1s. 9d. for each horse, according to the number of horses expressed by figures on such tickets, and in the receipt given for the same.

Every postmaster, &c. who shall let horses to hire by the mile or stage, to be used in travelling post, shall, previous to the letting such horse, ask, and receive of person hiring the same, one penny half-penny per mile for each mile such horse shall be so hired to travel, at the rate or number of miles which he shall charge such traveller for the stage or distance such horse may be hired to go, and shall at the same time he receives duty, deliver to the person hiring horse, one or more of said stamp-office tickets, and to which poſtmaſter, &c. ſhall add, if an innkeeper, name of his ſign or houſe, if not an innkeeper, his own name, and ſhall alſo inſert name of place where ſuch licenſed perſon reſides, and to which ſuch horſes may be hired to go, and if to London, name of ſtreet, ſquare, or place there, and in words or figures, month and day of month, with number of miles for which ſuch horſes are ſo hired; and if any perſon neglect to aſk and receive the ſaid duty of one penny halfpenny per mile from perſon hiring horſe, or neglect or refuſe to deliver tickets filled up to ſuch perſon ſo hiring horſes, he ſhall forfeit 10l. and moreover, in caſe of not receiving the ſaid duty, be chargeable therewith in the ſame manner as if actually received.

Every traveller to whom the tickets, whereon ſhall be expreſſed the number of miles, ſhall be delivered, if they ſhall paſs through any turnpike or toll barr, ſhall, at the firſt turnpike, toll-bar, or bridge at which any toll ſhall be by law collected, through which he ſhall paſs, deliver to the toll-gate keeper, ticket ſo given at place he hired horſe, which ſaid toll-gate keeper is to demand, receive and file; and if any traveller ſo going poſt ſhall have neglected to take ticket, or ſhall not deliver ſame properly filled up, he ſhall, before ſuch horſes be permitted to paſs through ſuch turnpike or toll bar, pay for every horſe hired and uſed by ſuch traveller 1s. 9d. which the gate-keeper is to aſk and demand, and not to permit horſe to paſs till paid the ſame, or produced ticket.

No traveller ſhall be compelled to pay for a greater number of miles than expreſſed upon the ticket iſſued to ſuch traveller; and if any perſon ſo licenced, ſhall inſert in any ſuch ticket name of any other place than to which the horſes ſhall be hired to go, or ſhall fill up a leſs number of miles than the number charged to ſuch traveller, every offender ſhall forfeit 10l. and licence may be refuſed him in future.

Where any ticket ſhall be iſſued, with the number of miles expreſſed thereon, and perſon ſo iſſuing the ſame, ſhall charge the traveller a ſpecific ſum by the ſtage, and not after uſual or certain rate per mile, perſon ſhall be accountable for one-fourth of the money ſo received as for duty, and ſhall expreſs on the ſaid ticket the money chargeed to ſuch traveller, and enter ſame in weekly account, one fourth part of the money ſo received and pay the ſame to the collector of the duties, and if any perſon ſhall act contrary hereto, he ſhall forfeit [illegible]

Every ſuch poſtmaſter ſhall previous to ſuch horſe being uſed, aſk and receive of perſon hiring the ſame, one penny halfpenny per mile for each mile ſuch horſe ſhall be ſo hired to go where the diſtance ſhall be aſcertained, and where the diſtance ſhall not be aſcertained 1s. 9d., and ſhall at the ſame time deliver to perſon ſo hiring horſe one or more of the ſtamp-office tickets, with the words [illegible] inſerted therein, as occaſion ſhall require, and to which every poſtmaſter, &c. ſhall add [illegible] innkeeper, the name of his ſign or houſe if not his own name, and ſhall alſo inſert name of the place where licenſed perſon reſides, and, in words or figures, the month and day thereof; and if any perſon ſhall neglect to aſk and receive the ſaid duty of one penny halfpenny per mile, or 1s. 9d. for each horſe from hirer, or not deliver ticket, to forfeit [illegible] and though not receiving duty, yet to be chargeable therewith.

Every perſon to whom day ticket is delivered, if he, in the courſe of the day, paſs through any turnpike, toll bar, or bridge (where toll is collected by law) ſhall, at the firſt through which he ſhall paſs, deliver to toll gatherer day tickets where he hired horſe which toll gatherer is to file, and in return for ſuch day ticket, perſon ſhall receive from toll-gatherer an *exchange ticket*, to be ſupplied from ſtamp-office, containing name of county in which the turnpike ſhall be and the words *received day ticket*) with number of horſes according to the figures in day ticket, with name of place at which ſuch ticket was given, and particular day in which ſuch exchange ticket was iſſued, in printed or written letters or figures, which ſaid exchange tickets toll-gatherer is to deliver *gratis*, in return for day ticket, ſaid exchange ticket to be ſhewn at every turnpike through which traveller ſhall afterwards on that day paſs with ſuch horſe; and if perſon to whom day ticket be delivered, ſhall not leave ſame at firſt turnpike, or refuſe to ſhew ticket given him in exchange at toll-bar, he ſhall pay for every horſe then uſed by him 1s. 9d. before horſe ſhall paſs; toll-gatherer to aſk and return ſame to his uſe; and where name of owner of carriage ſhall be marked on foot board, ſeat, pole, ſhaft or ſplinter-bar, when the carriage is let out to hire at the ſame time with the horſes, toll-gatherer ſhall not permit horſe to paſs through until traveller ſhall have paid the ſame, or left ſuch day ticket, or produced exchange ticket.

If any perſon ſhall take off the braſs or tin plate to evade duty, or payment of the 1s. 9d. for each horſe at the turnpike, he ſhall forfeit 10l.

In caſe any carriage ſhall paſs without having ſuch braſs or tin-plate affixed thereon, driver ſhall forfeit 40s.

Where any poſtmaſter, &c. ſhall let to hire any horſe to return in leſs time than two days, and the number of miles, inſtead of the words (*for a day*) ſhall be inſerted in ticket, he ſhall fill up the name of the place to which the horſes are hired to go, and the true number of miles, aſcertaining the diſtance both going to and returning from the place expreſſed in ticket, and in default of not filling up the ſaid ticket he ſhall forfeit 10l. and moreover be chargeable with the duty as if actually received.

Poſtmaſter, &c. when he ſhall let to hire for two days or longer horſes for drawing carriage on public road, ſhall deliver to the perſon travelling in carriage, or to driver, note or certificate to be ſupplied from the ſtamp-office, on which ſhall be the words (*hired for two or more days*) and to which poſtmaſter, &c. ſhall add the day of the month, name of place of his abode and number of days for which ſuch horſes ſhall be hired, and name and place of abode of perſon hiring ſame, and perſon travelling or driver ſhall, at the firſt turnpike or place where toll is by law collected, if he paſs through any, deliver to the toll gate keeper the note or certificate ſo given, which toll-gate keeper is to ask and receive and file; and in return for note or certificate the toll-gate keeper shall deliver a ticket (called the check ticket) from the stamp-office, which shall contain the name of the county in which the turnpike or toll-bar shall be, and the words (*certificate delivered*) and also the name of place whence note or certificate issued, together with mark denoting the particular day on which such check was issued, in printed or written letters or figures; which said check ticket the said toll-gate keeper is to deliver gratis in return for note or certificate, and which said check ticket shall be shewn by driver or person therein to the toll-gate keeper at every turnpike or toll-bar through which the said horses must pass; and if any person so hiring horses, shall have neglected to take such note or certificate, or shall neglect or refuse to leave the same at the turnpike or toll-bar, or shall refuse to shew at the several turnpikes or toll-bars through which he shall pass the check ticket so given him, traveller shall pay for every horse [illegible]d. before horses be permitted to pass such turnpike or toll-bar, which the said toll-gate keeper is to retain to his own use, and not permit horses to pass till travellers shall have paid the same, or produced such note, certificate or check ticket; and if postmaster, &c. shall insert in note or certificate any false or fictitious name or place of abode, or shall wilfully insert therein any fictitious name or place, or alter the name of any person hiring horses, or shall let out such horses, or pretend to let out horses for longer time than for which the same were actually hired, with intent to evade duty, such postmaster, &c. shall forfeit 20l. and the said commissioners may refuse to grant offender licence in future.

Horses hired for drawing carriage for less time than *[illegible] days* shall be deemed to be hired for a day, and shall be subject as such are by the act.

Every toll-gate keeper receiving day tickets or notes or certificates for two or more days, and shall refuse to give travellers tickets gratis in exchange, or deliver the exchange ticket or check ticket, without having received in lieu thereof the stamp-office ticket or note or certificate *for two or more days*, or shall make or permit to be made, alteration in tickets to be filed after the same shall have come to his custody, or shall deliver any tickets directed to be received and filed, to any person than duly authorised to receive same, he shall forfeit 40s.

Every postmaster, &c. so licenced, not residing within London or Westminster, or within the bills of mortality, shall, at such times and places as shall be directed, produce and deliver the accounts for the weeks ending on the Saturday preceding such delivery, and then be accounted for, under penalty of 10l. for every default, and double the amount of the money payable for said duties, for non-payment thereof.

Every postmaster, &c. so licenced, shall enter in his weekly account, the tickets, notes, or certificates so issued on days in which the same shall be issued; and if any postmaster, &c. shall date any of the posting tickets, or day tickets, or any note or certificate, otherwise than as the same shall at the time of such delivery be entered in his weekly account, shall forfeit 40s.

Every postmaster, &c. so licenced, who shall be guilty of wilful concealment, or making false accounts, or other fraudulent contrivance, device, or pretence whatsoever, with an intent to defraud, he shall forfeit 50l. and said commissioners may refuse to grant him licence in future.

In order to prevent the evading the payment of the duties under the pretence that the duty has been paid for the stage, and that the horses are on their return home, it is enacted, that the person taking the hire for such horses either by the mile or stage, shall be accountable for the duty due thereon.

In order to prevent the evading the payment of duties upon horses hired by the mile or stage, under pretence of such horses being let to hire for a day or less period of time, no person at whose inn, house, or place kept for letting horses to hire, travellers shall change horses, shall let to hire any horse to travellers otherwise than by the mile or stage; and if any post master, &c. shall not deliver ... ticket to ... travelling post, he shall forfeit 10l.

Every toll-gate keeper ... or ... receive from collectors to whom ... shall deliver the day tickets and posting tickets three pence ... pound sterling, which the duties upon ... shall amount unto ... after that rate for less sum; such allowance shall be over and above the privilege of retaining the money by him collected from the persons who shall not have delivered tickets to him.

Every toll-gate keeper shall ... the tickets received ... of the ... from the head office ... to such place ... collector shall require, and deliver up ... to such collector.

Toll-gate keepers who shall ... receive such ... tickets, who will not ... as aforesaid, shall, upon demand made ... at the ... gate of such turnpike ... or toll-bar, deliver such tickets to the collector; and if he refuse to deliver up such ... tickets so received, upon demand, he shall, for each ticket refused, forfeit ...

If toll-gate keeper shall ... wilfully ... or refuse to receive tickets ... or shall ... to ... refuse to ... the same ... he shall forfeit ...

In case any toll-gate keeper shall ... or take less money than ... specified, he shall forfeit ...

Commissioners of stamp-duties may erect ... in any public road ... for the receipt of ... tickets, and place persons there ... who shall ... commissioners to collect ... tickets ... or ... to ... and to demand the money from the travellers for not producing ... the ... as the turnpike ... and be liable and subject ...

Every horse ... by the mile or stage shall be deemed to be hired to travel post ... though the person hiring the same do not ... travel ... stages upon post roads ... and although ... the stage or place ... to which such horse shall be hired, there shall not ... be ...

a[illegible]d [illegible] sh[illegible] [illegible] th[illegible] [illegible] c[illegible] th[illegible] road upon wh[illegible] such horses shall b[illegible] hired to go

---

S[illegible]age Coach[illegible] D[illegible]

I[illegible] person who shall keep any coach [illegible] [illegible] [illegible] [illegible] [illegible] [illegible] with four [illegible] [illegible] coach, [illegible] [illegible] [illegible] [illegible] [illegible] [illegible] shall [illegible] [illegible] [illegible] [illegible] fare [illegible] [illegible] [illegible] [illegible] shall forfeit, for ev[illegible] [illegible] time such coach, d[illegible] [illegible] [illegible] [illegible] [illegible] shall [illegible] [illegible] 10l.

No [illegible] [illegible] [illegible] [illegible] shall [illegible] [illegible] [illegible] coach [illegible] [illegible] more [illegible] coach [illegible] [illegible] [illegible]

Every perf[illegible] l[illegible]ensed to use any coach, [illegible] or carriages [illegible] to be employed as public stage coaches, shall pa[illegible] [illegible] [illegible] [illegible] such coach [illegible] other carriage shall be [illegible] used [illegible]

Eve[illegible] person so li[illegible] [illegible] [illegible] shall [illegible] at the time o[illegible] [illegible] [illegible] [illegible] [illegible] [illegible] to w[illegible] [illegible] [illegible] [illegible] [illegible] [illegible] [illegible] [illegible] [illegible] [illegible] number of miles [illegible] [illegible] [illegible] such coach [illegible] [illegible] [illegible] [illegible] [illegible] [illegible] [illegible] [illegible] [illegible] [illegible] b[illegible] inferred [illegible] [illegible] may

[illegible] [illegible] shall [illegible] [illegible] [illegible] [illegible] door, [illegible] the [illegible] [illegible] [illegible] [illegible] [illegible] [illegible] [illegible] [illegible] [illegible] [illegible] [illegible] length [illegible] [illegible]

[illegible] proprietor of a[illegible] [illegible] [illegible] [illegible] use of the [illegible] shall gi[illegible] notice in writ[illegible] [illegible] seven days at least, [illegible]

[illegible] the fam[illegible] shall have such [illegible] the back of his [illegible] word [illegible] [illegible] ours, [illegible] be [illegible]

[illegible] performing [illegible] [illegible] [illegible] publish[illegible] [illegible]

[illegible] [illegible] in the supreme court [illegible] who[illegible] [illegible] witnesses [illegible] and summons [illegible] with the book [illegible]

[illegible] passengers on [illegible] 2[illegible]

SERVANTS.

Inh[illegible]

[illegible] Geo. III. [illegible]

By th[illegible] all the former duties on servants are re[illegible] [illegible] and the following to [illegible] from the 5th of July, 1[illegible]

Male servants.

For [illegible] *per ann*[illegible]

[illegible] more than [illegible] each

[illegible] than [illegible]

[illegible] greater number [illegible] each

The duties on men servants are to extend to persons of the following description, employed in the following capacities: viz. Maitre d'hotel, House-steward, [illegible] of the [illegible] room of the Chamber, Valet de Chambre, Butler, Under Butler, Clerk of the Kitchen, [illegible] Cook, House-Porter, [illegible] Footman, Coachman, Groom,

Postilion, Stable Boy, [illegible] Stables, Gardener [illegible] [illegible] [illegible] Coffee-houses [illegible] Auction [illegible] other [illegible] retail (other [illegible] Waiters) or [illegible] for [illegible] names [illegible] servants really [illegible] any of the [illegible] [illegible], even [illegible] except [illegible] [illegible] paid for [illegible] on the master by magistrates, [illegible]

[illegible] persons [illegible] exceed [illegible] Footmen, [illegible] [illegible] said [illegible] liveries

[illegible] Footmen, or Helpers let out [illegible] shall be paid for by those who employ [illegible] [illegible] who shall contract [illegible] [illegible] shall be paid for by the persons who employ them

[illegible] Servants

For [illegible] [illegible], *per annum*, 2s 6d

[illegible]

[illegible] [illegible] [illegible]

[illegible] officers [illegible] deliver to the [illegible] [illegible] and [illegible] of their [illegible] [illegible] [illegible] [illegible] [illegible] [illegible] for [illegible] [illegible] [illegible] the [illegible] [illegible] refusal or neglect [illegible] [illegible] shall [illegible] power to [illegible] from the best information they can get, and [illegible] [illegible] shall be [illegible] [illegible] unless [illegible] [illegible] to the commissioners for such [illegible] as they shall

* *Female servants are [illegible], and [illegible] are exempt [illegible] [illegible] [illegible] the am-[illegible]*

think reasonable, but if they refuse or neglect [illegible] within [illegible], the parties so refusing shall forfeit [illegible] [illegible]. Where the persons giving such lists have servants at different places, they must mention all the [illegible] [illegible] to pay for at every other place mentioned [illegible] [illegible] other circumstances relative to the situation of each place, in order to their being fairly rated according to the whole number.

Masters or mistresses omitting the names or number of any of their servants, to be charged double for every such omission. Half to the informer.

Persons letting lodgings must give a list of the number of servants of both sexes kept by each lodger [illegible] [illegible] [illegible] [illegible] required, with the christian and surnames of such lodgers and inmates, and their servants also, to the best of their knowledge, or forfeit [illegible].

Appeals must be made to the commissioners, or persons dissatisfied with their [illegible] [illegible] [illegible] to the Court of King's Bench in England, or the Court of Session in Scotland.

Exemption.

Servants employed in husbandry, manufactures, or trade, or by and within the Universities [illegible] in England or Scotland [illegible] [illegible] [illegible] Colleges [illegible] [illegible] [illegible] or [illegible] [illegible] or by any of the Royal Family, or by [illegible] [illegible], or Foreign [illegible] [illegible] [illegible] [illegible] of the Royal Hospitals [illegible] [illegible] [illegible] [illegible] [illegible] Bridewell, Bethlem, St. [illegible] [illegible] [illegible] the Foundling Hospital.

Any officer of [illegible] [illegible] dragoons, under the [illegible], or not receiving the pay of a field officer, [illegible] [illegible] [illegible] [illegible] servant [illegible] shall be exempt from the duty, whether such servant [illegible] [illegible] his re[illegible] [illegible] or not.

Every officer, without distinction, in the land service, of every description, including marines, who employs one soldier of the regiment or company to which he belongs as a servant, and every officer in the navy under the rank of a master and commander, in actual service, who employs one sailor [illegible] [illegible], that is actually borne upon the books of the office to which such officer belongs, are for such servants exempt from this duty.

Officers on half-pay, disabled, either in the army, navy, or marines, are not liable to this duty for one male servant only.

Any family having two or more children or grandchildren living, legitimately begotten, under 14 years of age, are allowed to keep one female servant not liable to the duty; if they have four children, they are allowed two female servants free of duty, if six, three such servants, and in the same proportion for every two children of the above description.

A family having thus [illegible] children of the above description, the servant or servants who are not exempted, are to be rated as if there were no other in the house, that is, where there happens to be three female servants, and on account of four children, two are exempted, the third is only to be charged half-a-crown. This example will serve for all others.

Female servants under fourteen years of age, and above sixty, are not liable to this duty, neither are dairy-maids.

Window and house tax collectors are to collect these duties likewise.

Bachelors.

Every man of the age of twenty-one years and upwards, never having been married, who shall keep one male servant or more, shall pay £1. 5s for each, over and above the duties before mentioned. 25 Geo. III. c. 41.

Every man of the age of twenty-one years and upwards, never having been married, keeping one female servant, shall pay 2s. 6d. in addition to the former 2s. 6.

Five Shillings in addition for each if he has two female servants.

And 10s in addition for each for three or more female servants.

AUCTIONEERS AND AUCTIONS

EVERY Auctioneer residing within the bills of mortality must take out an annual licence at the Excise Office, for which he is to pay 20s. with three and per cent. thereon, 1l. 3s. and without the bills, 5s. with the three and per cent. [illegible] for which he must apply to the collectors and supervisors within the district where he lives, under the penalty of 100l. in London, and [illegible] in the country. Sworn brokers admitted by the Lord Mayor and Court of Aldermen of London are to pay only 5s. for their licence. (17 Geo. III. c. 50.)

Three pence halfpenny to be paid in the pound upon all goods sold by auction of the following description, viz. any interest in reversion or possession in any freehold, copyhold, or leasehold lands, tenements, houses, or hereditaments, and on any annuities or sums of money charged thereon, and of any utensils in husbandry and farming stock, ships, and vessels, and of any reversion or interest in the public funds, also plate and jewels. ([illegible] Geo. III. c. 13.)

Seven pence to be paid in the pound upon all goods of the following description, viz. fixtures, furniture, pictures, books, [illegible], carriages, and all other goods and chattels whatsoever, except such as are hereafter exempted. (2[illegible] Geo. III. c. 1[illegible].)

The above duties are charged upon the auctioneer (not the purchaser) for which he must stand bound for [illegible] with two sureties, to pay within [illegible] days after each sale, the amount of the said duties, which he must state upon oath. In the country six weeks are allowed to pay in the duty. (17 Geo. III. c. 50.)

Two days previous notice of every sale, with an attested catalogue, to be sent to the Excise Office, mentioning where and when the sale is to be made, or forfeit [illegible]. Three days previous notice in the country.

Exemptions.

These duties not to extend to goods or estates sold by order, or under decrees of the Court of Chancery, or Exchequer, or Commissioners of Customs, Excise, Board of Ordnance, Great Sessions or Exchequer in Wales or Scotland, East India Company, Navy or Victualling Office; goods distrained for rent or tythes; or sales on account of lords or ladies of any manor for granting copyhold or customary estates, leases, &c. for lives or years, or under the authority [illegible] the benefit of creditors, or the effects of bankrupts sold by assignees; or goods imported by way of merchandise from any British colony or plantation in America, provided it is the manufacture or growth of that colony, and really sold for the benefit of the original importer, to whom they were consigned, and the sale is within twelve months after their arrival here; or goods wrecked or stranded, if sold for the benefit of the insurers or proprietors; or goods damaged by fire, if sold for the benefit of the insurer or insurers. Corn, hay, grass, dung, live or dead stock, or any kind of produce which is sold upon the estate where it grew, are also exempt, if sold by the owner of such estate. The unmanufactured produce of mines is likewise exempt, if sold by the proprietor of the mine.

Additional Exemptions, by 29 Geo. III. c. 63.

From the 1st of October, 1780, all goods woven or fabricated in the looms of this kingdom, which shall be sold in the entire pieces in which the same shall be taken from the loom, and in lots of the price of [illegible] or upwards, shall not pay the auction duty imposed by the act of the 17th of Geo. III. but [illegible] than entire pieces, [illegible] unless the goods were [illegible] ed at the sale.

The auctioneer to give security, beside the bond directed in the 17th, in the sum of [illegible] with two sureties at least, that he will, within fourteen days after such sale, deliver to the next office of excise a particular account of all the several lots so sold, the amount of the money bid, and the price of each, and that he will not knowingly put up for sale any piece or other goods of foreign manufacture, or any goods of English manufacture, except in the quantity in which the same were taken from the loom, without charging the duties imposed by 17 Geo. III.

More Exemptions by 30 Geo. III c. 26.

Any goods imported into this kingdom, by way of merchandize, from the settlement of Yucatan, in South America, shall be free from the duty on the first sale of such goods at auction by the original importer to whom the same was consigned, and by whom they were entered at the custom-house at the port of importation so as such sale shall be made within twelve months after such goods shall be imported, by some licenced auctioneer

---

TOBACCO AND SNUFF

(29 Geo III c 68 and 30 Geo III c 40 consolidated.)

MANUFACTURERS and dealers are, three days before beginning to manufacture or sell any tobacco tobacco stalks Spanish tobacco stalks for tobacco stalk flour snuff-work tobacco stalk flour, or snuff, to make entry in writing [illegible] of all the premises used by them in the manufacture [illegible] sale or keeping [illegible] of the above articles [illegible] office of Excise within the limits of such premises on pain of 200l. for every part not entered, with all articles found therein and the packages

Persons making entry must occupy a house of 10l. rent and pay to church and poor

Manufacturers or dealers are to have the words *Manufacturer of and Dealer in Tobacco and Snuff* or *Tobacco, or Snuff*, or *Manufacturer of or Dealer in Tobacco and Snuff*, or *Tobacco or Snuff* in large characters on the outer door [illegible] in the [illegible], or in some conspicuous part of every room or other place used by them in the manufacturing keeping, or selling any of the above articles, on pain of 50l.

Any person having such words without entry forfeits 100l

Dealers in tobacco or snuff, are to take out licence before dealing in the same paying 5s. for a licence to deal in tobacco or snuff, within the limits of the of fices in London, or Edinburgh and 2s. 6d. for such licence in any other part of Great Britain. To be renewed annually on pain of [illegible]

Manufacturers of Tobacco and Snuff are required to take out licences, which are to be granted as follows, viz:

[illegible] manufacturers of tobacco and snuff after [illegible] November 1791, who within the [illegible] preceding the [illegible] October [illegible] to the taking out of the licence, did not weigh out for manufacture, [illegible] directions of this act, more tobacco and snuff [illegible] than [illegible] lb. weight, — — — — £ [illegible]

More than 20,000,	and less than [illegible],	—	3 [illegible]
More than 35,000,	and less than [illegible],	—	[illegible]
More than 40,000,	and less than [illegible]	—	[illegible]
More than 50,000,	and less than [illegible],	—	6 [illegible]
More than 60,000,	and less than [illegible],	—	[illegible]
More than [illegible]	and less than 80,000	—	8 [illegible]
More than 8[illegible]	and less than [illegible]	—	[illegible]
More than 90,000,	and less than [illegible],	—	10 [illegible]
More than 100,000,	and less than [illegible],	—	[illegible]
More than 120,000,	and less than [illegible]	—	[illegible]
More than 150,000,	— — — — —	—	[illegible]

Licenced manufacturers selling tobacco and snuff at any time in quantities not less than 4 lb. and [illegible] not less than 2 lb. need not take out the dealers licence.

Tobacco and snuff cannot be imported into any other port of Great Britain than the [illegible] port of [illegible] [illegible] [illegible] *Falmouth*, [illegible] *Hull*, [illegible] Greenock, *and Leith*, on pain of the forfeiture of the vessel.

No person [illegible] up or begin any manufacture of tobacco or snuff [illegible] places less than five miles distant from any part of the sea-coast of Great Britain, except in the ports and places mentioned above, and within three miles of the same, and also except in cities [illegible] their suburbs, [illegible] market towns [illegible] [illegible] of any place contrary [illegible] be valid.

HOUSES.

A Table of the Duty upon Houses.

(19 Geo. III. c. 59.)

Rent	At per Pound		Total per Yr			Rent	At per Pound		Total per Yr		
l.	s.	d.	l.	s.	d.	L.	s.	d.	l.	s.	d.
5	0	6	0	2	6	23	0	9	0	17	3
6	——		0	3	0	24	——		0	18	0
7	——		0	3	6	25	——		0	18	9
8	——		0	4	0	26	——		0	19	6
9	——		0	4	6	27	——		1	0	3
10	——		0	5	0	28	——		1	1	0
11	——		0	5	6	29	——		1	1	9
12	——		0	6	0	30	——		1	2	6
13	——		0	6	6	31	——		1	3	3
14	——		0	7	0	32	——		1	4	0
15	——		0	7	6	33	——		1	4	9
16	——		0	8	0	34	——		1	5	6
17	——		0	8	6	35	——		1	6	3
18	——		0	9	0	36	——		1	7	0
19	——		0	9	6	37	——		1	7	9
20	0	9	0	15	0	38	——		1	8	6
21	——		0	15	9	39	——		1	9	3
22	——		0	16	6	40	1	0	2	0	0

And so on at the same rate of 1s. in the Pound for a rent of any amount.

Clauses relative to the House Tax.

The offices, yards, gardens, coach-houses, brew-houses, wood houses, wash houses, &c. provided they all stand within the compass of one acre, belonging to the dwelling house, must be valued with the dwelling house, and be liable to the same duties.

Shops and warehouses are also liable, if attached to the dwelling houses, except those of wharfingers.

No warehouse that is a distinct building is liable.

No house to be deemed occupied where one person is only left in charge of it.

Where houses are let in tenements, the landlords must pay the duty.

Halls and offices that pay other taxes are liable to this.

Farm houses used only for husbandry under [illegible] per annum, are not chargeable, nor are houses for the reception of poor or if not occupied by the owner, or rented by a tenant.

WINDOWS

BY 6 Geo. III c. 38 there shall be paid for every dwelling house inhabited within England the yearly sum of 3s. and by 24 Geo. III c. 38, an additional 3s. in the whole six shillings.

And if such house contains seven windows or upwards, duties are payable for such windows according to the following tables.

Accurate Tables of all the present Window duties including the 3s. by 6th of Geo. III c. 38, and the 3s. by 24th of Geo. III c. 38 with their whole amount in the last column.

Note.—These tables are calculated for the duties payable in England; those which are raised in Scotland commences at six Windows, which are taxed 1s. and every subsequent number, is 3s. less than the total amount in the following tables. For instance seven windows in Scotland is 8s. 2d. eight Windows is 13s. and so on through the whole.

Number of Windows	Old Tax			New Tax.			Amount of both		
Assessed for	£	s	d	£	s	d	£	s	d
7	0	4	0	0	9	0	0	[illegible]	[illegible]
8	0	7	0	0	11	0	0	18	0
9	0	9	0	0	1[illegible]	6	1	2	6
10	0	1[illegible]	4	0	15	0	1	[illegible]	4
11	0	14	0	0	18	6	1	12	6
12	0	17	0	1	1	0	1	18	0
13	1	0	4	1	[illegible]	0	2	[illegible]	4
14	1	4	0	1	8	0	2	1[illegible]	0
15	1	[illegible]	0	1	13	0	2	18	6
16	1	[illegible]	[illegible]	1	18	0	3	5	0
17	1	8	0	2	3	0	[illegible]	11	0
18	1	10	0	2	[illegible]	0	[illegible]	18	0
19	1	11	6	2	1[illegible]	0	4	4	6
20	1	14	8	2	18	0	4	12	8
21	1	18	0	3	3	0	5	1	0
22	[illegible]	1	6	3	[illegible]	0	[illegible]	9	6
23	2	[illegible]	0	3	1[illegible]	0	[illegible]	1[illegible]	2
24	2	9	0	3	18	0	6	7	0
*25	2	1[illegible]	0	4	3	0	6	16	0
26	2	1[illegible]	0				6	18	0
27	2	1[illegible]	0	4	3	0	7	[illegible]	0
28	2	19	0				7	2	0
29	3	1	0				7	[illegible]	0
30	3	[illegible]	0				7	1[illegible]	0
31	3	[illegible]	0				7	18	0
32	3	[illegible]	0	4	13	0	8	0	0
33	[illegible]	9	0				8	2	0
34	3	11	0				8	[illegible]	0
35	[illegible]	1[illegible]	0				8	1[illegible]	0
36	[illegible]	1[illegible]	0				8	13	0
37	[illegible]	17	0	5	3	0	9	0	0
38	3	19	0				9	2	0
39	4	1	0				9	4	0

* The Old Duty is Two Shillings for every Window above Twenty-five, and Three Shillings for the House.

Numb. of Windows	Old Tax £	s	d	New Tax £	s	d	Amount of both £	s	d
40	4	3	[illegible]				[illegible]	1[illegible]	0
41	4	[illegible]	0				[illegible]	18	0
42	4	[illegible]	0	[illegible]	1[illegible]	0	10	0	[illegible]
43	4	9	0				10	[illegible]	[illegible]
44	4	11	[illegible]				10	4	
45	4	[illegible]	[illegible]				1[illegible]	1[illegible]	[illegible]
46	4	[illegible]	[illegible]				[illegible]	18	
47	4	17	0	6	3	[illegible]	11	0	0
48	4	1[illegible]	[illegible]				11	2	0
49	[illegible]	1	0				11	1	0
50	5	3	0				11	16	0
51	5	[illegible]	0				11	18	0
52	5	[illegible]	0	6	13	0	12	0	0
53	5	[illegible]	0				12	[illegible]	0
54	5	11	[illegible]				12	1	0
55	5	1[illegible]	0				12	16	
56	5	1[illegible]	0				1[illegible]	1[illegible]	0
57	[illegible]		0	7	3	0	13	0	0
58	5	19	0				1[illegible]	2	0
59	6	1	[illegible]				13	[illegible]	0
60	6	[illegible]	0				1[illegible]	16	0
61	6	[illegible]	0				13	18	0
62	6	[illegible]	0	7	13	0	14	0	0
63	6	9	0				14	[illegible]	0
64	6	11	0				14	4	0
65	6	13	0				1[illegible]	16	0
66	6	1[illegible]	0				14	18	0
67	6	17	0	8	3	0	1[illegible]	0	0
68	6	1[illegible]	0				1[illegible]	[illegible]	0
69	[illegible]	1	0				1[illegible]	4	
70	[illegible]		0				1[illegible]	16	0
71	7		0				1[illegible]	1[illegible]	[illegible]
72	7	[illegible]	0	8	1[illegible]	0	1[illegible]	0	0
73	[illegible]	9	0				16	2	0
74	[illegible]	11	0						
75	7	1[illegible]	0				1[illegible]	1[illegible]	0
76	7	1[illegible]	0	9	3	0	1[illegible]	1[illegible]	0
77	7	17	0				17	0	0

Numb. of Windows	Old Tax	New Tax	Amount of [illegible]
	£ s d	£ s d	£ s d
[illegible]0	[illegible]	9 3 [illegible]	1[illegible]
[illegible]	8 1		1 4 [illegible]
[illegible]	8 [illegible]		1 1 [illegible]
1	[illegible]		1[illegible]
[illegible]	[illegible]	9 1 [illegible]	1[illegible]
[illegible]3	8 [illegible]		1 [illegible]
[illegible]4	[illegible] 11		1 [illegible]
[illegible]	[illegible] 1[illegible]		1 [illegible]
[illegible]6	1	10 3	
[illegible]	1[illegible]		1[illegible]
[illegible]	[illegible]		1[illegible] 0
8[illegible]	9 1 0		1[illegible] 0
[illegible]	9 [illegible]		[illegible] 1 [illegible]
1	9 [illegible]	1[illegible] 1[illegible] 0	1[illegible] 18 [illegible]
[illegible]	9 [illegible]		1 [illegible] 0
[illegible]3	9 [illegible] 0		2 [illegible]
[illegible]	1		4 [illegible]
[illegible]	9 1[illegible]		
[illegible]6	9 1 0	11 3 [illegible]	2[illegible] 1[illegible]
97	9 1[illegible]		21 0 0
98	9 10		21 [illegible]
[illegible]9	10 1		[illegible]
1[illegible]	10 2		6 [illegible]
101	10 [illegible]		2[illegible]
102	10 7 0		1 [illegible]
103	10 [illegible]		2 12
104	10 11	1[illegible] 3 0	1 [illegible]
1[illegible]	10 13		2 16
[illegible]	10 15		2[illegible] 18
107	10 17		[illegible]
1[illegible]8	10 19		2 [illegible]
1[illegible]9	11 1		[illegible]
110	11 [illegible] 0		[illegible]
1[illegible]1	11 [illegible]		[illegible]
[illegible]12	11 [illegible]	1[illegible] 3 0	[illegible]
113	1[illegible]		1[illegible]
1[illegible]4	11 11		[illegible]
1[illegible]	11 13 0		[illegible] 16

Numb. of Windows	Old Tax £	s	d	New Tax £	s	d	Amount of both £	s	d
116	11	1	0				[illegible]	18	0
117	11	1	0	13	3	0	[illegible]	0	0
118	11	1[illegible]	0				[illegible]	2	0
119	1[illegible]	1	0				[illegible]	4	0
120	1[illegible]	[illegible]	0				[illegible]	[illegible]	0
121	1[illegible]	[illegible]	[illegible]				[illegible]	8	0
122	1[illegible]	[illegible]	[illegible]				[illegible]	1[illegible]	0
123	1[illegible]	[illegible]	[illegible]				[illegible]	1[illegible]	0
124	1[illegible]	11	0				[illegible]	1[illegible]	0
125	1[illegible]	1	0	14	3	0	[illegible]	1[illegible]	0
126	1[illegible]	1	0				2[illegible]	13	0
127	1[illegible]	1	0				[illegible]	0	0
128	12	19	0				7	2	0
129	13	[illegible]	[illegible]				[illegible]	4	0
130	1[illegible]	[illegible]	0				[illegible]	6	0
131	1[illegible]	[illegible]	[illegible]				[illegible]	8	0
132	[illegible]	[illegible]	0				[illegible]	10	0
133	1[illegible]	9	0				[illegible]	1[illegible]	0
134	1[illegible]	11	0				[illegible]	1[illegible]	0
135	13	1[illegible]	0	15	3	0	[illegible]	16	0
136	1[illegible]	1[illegible]	[illegible]				[illegible]	1[illegible]	0
137	1[illegible]	17	0				[illegible]	0	0
138	1[illegible]	19	0				[illegible]	2	0
139	1[illegible]	1	0				[illegible]	4	0
140	[illegible]	[illegible]	[illegible]				[illegible]	6	0
141	14	[illegible]	[illegible]				[illegible]	8	0
142	14	[illegible]	0				[illegible]	10	0
143	1[illegible]	9	0				[illegible]	1[illegible]	0
144	1[illegible]	11	0				3[illegible]	1[illegible]	[illegible]
145	1[illegible]	1	[illegible]	16	3	0	[illegible]	1[illegible]	0
146	1[illegible]	1	0				3[illegible]	1[illegible]	0
147	1[illegible]	1	[illegible]				[illegible]	0	0
148	1[illegible]	1[illegible]	0				[illegible]	2	0
149	1[illegible]	1	0				[illegible]	4	0
150	1[illegible]	[illegible]	[illegible]				[illegible]	6	0
151	1[illegible]	[illegible]	[illegible]				[illegible]	8	0
152	1[illegible]	7	0	17	3	0	32	10	0
153	1[illegible]	9	0				32	12	0

Numb of Windows.	Old Tax.	New Tax	Amount of [illegible]
	£ [illegible] d	£ s d	£ s d
[illegible]	[illegible] 11 0		[illegible] 13 0
[illegible]	[illegible] 1[illegible] 0		16
[illegible]	[illegible] 1 0	1[illegible] 3 0	13 [illegible]
[illegible]	[illegible]		[illegible] 0
[illegible]	[illegible] 1[illegible] 0		[illegible] 0
[illegible]	[illegible] 1 0		[illegible] 0
160	[illegible] 3 [illegible]		[illegible] 0
161	16 [illegible] 0		[illegible]
[illegible]	16 [illegible] 0		[illegible]
163	16 9 0		[illegible] 0
[illegible]	16 11 0	18 3 0	[illegible] 0
[illegible]	16 13 0		[illegible] 0
[illegible]	[illegible] 1[illegible] 0		[illegible] 15 0
[illegible]	[illegible]		0 0
[illegible]	1[illegible] 19 0		[illegible] 2 0
[illegible]	17 1 0		4 [illegible]
[illegible]	17 3 0		[illegible] 6 0
[illegible]	17 5 [illegible]		8 0
[illegible]	17 [illegible] 0		[illegible] 0
173	17 9 0		[illegible] 12 0
174	17 11 0	19 3 0	[illegible] 0
[illegible]	17 1[illegible] 0		[illegible] 16 0
[illegible]	17 1[illegible] 0		[illegible] 0
[illegible]	17 17 0		[illegible]7 0 0
[illegible]	17 19 0		[illegible]
[illegible]	18 1 0		[illegible] 0
180	18 3 0	[illegible] 3 0 *.*	[illegible] 0 0

. The new Tax on one Houf[illegible] not exceed [illegible] notwithftanding [illegible] number of Windows [illegible] be [illegible] the old [illegible] Five Shillings [illegible] before mentioned for any number of Windows [illegible] without limitation to which is to be added the old Duty [illegible] upon the Houfe.

Perfons occupying three or more Houfes to pay only for thofe two which contain [illegible] of Windows [illegible] on giving notice thereof to the collectors [illegible] and persons neglecting to pay according to such [illegible] pe[illegible] [illegible]—Where Houses are let in different Tenements the Landlord shall be deemed the [illegible]—Poor people exempted from [illegible] Poor [illegible] are [illegible]—Dwelling rooms in other [illegible] to other [illegible] or Parish [illegible] to be subject to the Pu[illegible] [illegible]—Apartments [illegible] the Inn of Court [illegible]—Not to extend to any House belonging to the Royal Family—Work-houses are also exempted [illegible] Charity Schools and Houses provided for the Relief of poor persons [illegible] Hospitals except Apartments for Officers [illegible] [illegible] chargeable to pay for [illegible]—[illegible] three or more Windows, separated by [illegible] less than twelve Inches [illegible] charged [illegible] one Window—Where any number of Windows are separated by [illegible] or [illegible] kind of [illegible] or Separation [illegible] more or less than twelve Inches each Window [illegible] Door or Fan [illegible] shall be deemed as separate Windows, and will be charged as such.

Note Persons who [illegible] Chambers in any Inns [illegible] Court are to pay One Shilling for every Window, exclusive of the New Duty

RUNNING HORSES AND HORSE DEALERS.

([illegible] Geo. III c [illegible])

FOR every horse [illegible] to start or run for any plate [illegible] prize sum of money or any thing whatsoever, in addition to the duties of former and subsequent acts laid upon horses the further sum of [illegible]

And the owner of every such horse shall previously pay the sum of [illegible] to the Clerk of the Course or other person authorised to make the entry [illegible] if he shall neglect or refuse to pay, he shall forfeit 20l.

And the Clerk of the Court shall within fourteen days after the receipt thereof give an account [illegible] and pay the sum to the Distributor of the Stamps, [illegible] on pain of 100l. for [illegible] such account, and [illegible] the money [illegible] at the time of such [illegible] and [illegible] thereafter [illegible] shall [illegible] for all monies accounted for and paid by him.

[illegible]

[illegible]

Any Justice [illegible] committed [illegible]

Persons [illegible] the next [illegible] the penalty [illegible]

BREWERS

(24 Geo. III. c. 41.)

EVERY common brewer of small or table beer, not being a common brewer of strong beer, shall take out an Excise licence annually, and pay for the same the sum of 1l. on penalty of 10l.

Every common brewer who shall brew strong beer shall, on penalty of 50l. take out a licence annually, and pay for the same the sum of 1l. 10s. if the quantity of beer brewed by him shall not exceed, within the year ending the 5th day of July in each year previous to his taking out the licence, the quantity of 1000 barrels.

Ditto, between 1000 and 2000 barrels, 2l.
Ditto, between 2000 and 5000, 5l.
Ditto between 5000 and 7500, 7l. 10s.
Ditto between 7500 and 10,000, 10l.
Ditto between 10,000 and 20,000, 20l.
Ditto, between 20,000 and 30,000, 30l.
Ditto between 30,000 and 40,000, 40l.
Ditto exceeding — — 40,000, 50l.

Brewers who withdraw their entries and make fresh ones, to pay the whole duty.

COACH MAKERS

(25 Geo. III. c. 49.)

EVERY maker of coaches, chaises, chariots, &c. must take out at the Excise Office in London, or of the [agents] in the country, including Scotland, a licence to be renewed annually at least ten days before the expiration of the former, for which they must pay 20s.

They must also pay 20s. duty for every four-wheel carriage newly built for sale, and 10s. for every two-wheel carriage. [illegible] Geo. III. c. 13.

These duties are also payable to the commissioners of the excise in town, or their agents in the country.

The duties are to be paid every six weeks and in order to ascertain the amount ... must be delivered ... distinguishing ... qualities of the carriages made within ... these ... set ... or sold ... and these ... ts must be sworn to by the master or chief workman.

ABSTRACT OF THE NEW ACT OF PARLIAMENT ...

... 5 Geo. III ... pealed.

... of Exchange.

FOR every Bill of Exchange, Draft or Order payable otherwise than on demand ... Promissory or other Note payable ... to the bearer on demand ... stamp duty as follows:

... the sum ... amount ...

... and not exceeding 30l. — Sixpence.
Above 30l. and not exceeding 50l. — Ninepence.
Above 50l. and not exceeding ...l. — One shilling.
Above ...l. and not exceeding ...l. — ...
Above ...l. and upwards — Two shillings.

... Bills of Exchange ...

(... Bills drawn ... Foreign Countries.)

For ... Bill of Exchange drawn in sets according to the custom of merchants, a stamp duty as follows:

Where the sum shall not exceed ...

...100l. — Sixpence.
Exceeding ...l. and not ...l. — Ninepence.
Exceeding ... — One shilling.
... each bill of each set so drawn ... declared to be ... with the duty.

... from the foregoing duties.

1. Drafts or Orders payable to the bearer on demand, bearing date on or before the day on which

the same shall be issued, and at the place from whence the same shall be drawn and issued, and drawn upon any Banker or person acting as a banker, and residing and transacting business as a banker, within ten miles of the place where such Draft or Order shall be actually drawn and issued

2. All Notes and Bills whatever issued by the Bank of England upon condition of their paying into the Exchequer the annual sum of 12,000l half yearly, on October 10, and April 5.

Regulations in the aforesaid act.

If any Bill, &c. shall be written on paper not stamped, or stamped with a stamp of lower value than directed, then there shall be due and paid the full duty thereby chargeable, which shall be payable by, and charged upon, all persons who shall draw or make and utter and negotiate such Bills, &c. And all persons who shall write or sign, or cause to be written or signed, or who shall accept or pay, or cause to be accepted or paid, any Bill, &c. without being first stamped with a proper stamp, or *upon which there shall not be some stamp resembling the same*, shall forfeit [illegible]

Every promissory or other note, payable to the bearer on demand, which shall be issued after payment under this act, shall notwithstanding be payable to the person holding the same, and such person may maintain an action thereupon

That no bill, &c. shall be available in law or equity, unless stamped with the lawful stamp, and that it shall *not be lawful for the Commissioners to stamp* any paper, &c. after any bill, &c. shall be written thereon, under any pretence whatever

Promissory Notes

For every piece of vellum, parchment, or paper upon which any bill of exchange, draft, or order for the payment of money on demand, shall be written or engrossed, &c. a stamp duty as follows, *viz*

Where the sum amounts to

2l. and not exceeding 5l. 5s.—Threepence.
Above 5l. 5s. and not exceeding 30l. —Sixpence.
Above 30l. and not exceeding 50l. —Ninepence.
Above 50l. and not exceeding 100l. —One shilling.
Above 100l. and not exceeding 200l. —1s. 6d.

Promissory Notes which are re-issued after payment at the place where first issued

For every promissory or other note for payment of money to the bearer on demand, which may be re-issued after payment at the place where the same was first issued, a stamp duty as follows, —

Where the sum amounts to

2l. and not exceeding 5l. 5s.—Threepence.
Above 5l. 5s. and not exceeding 30l. —Sixpence.
Above 30l. and not exceeding 50l. —Ninepence.
Above 50l. and not exceeding 100l. —One shilling.
Above 100l. and not exceeding 200l. —1s. 6d.

Where these promissory notes shall be paid by the person by whom the same shall have been [illegible] and re-issued [illegible] at the place where the [illegible] [illegible] Notes [illegible] than the sum [illegible] or [illegible] place [illegible] payment thereof, shall, after payment thereof, or refuse to cancel the same, such person shall [illegible]

20l. And if fuch Note fhall not be cancelled then and as often as it fhall be again iffued, there fhall be due, anfwered and paid, the like duty as was firft charged on fuch Note to be payable by and charged on, the perfon who fhall again iffue and negotiate fuch Note

Promiffory Notes which may be re-iffued after payment without reftriction to place

For any promiffory or other Note, payable to the bearer on demand, which may be re-iffued, after payment at the fame or any other place than where firft iffued, a ftamp duty as follows, viz

Where the fum amounts to

[illegible]l and not exceeding 5l 5s.—Sixpence
Above 5l 5s. and not exceeding 30l. —One fhilling

It is declared that thefe Notes may, as often as occafion fhall require, be again iffued by the perfon making the fame, notwithftanding fuch Notes have been paid by the perfon making the fame, or any other perfon in purfuance of any appointment for the payment thereof

⁂ All which d[illegible] fhall be paid by the perfon making or figning fuch Bills

Receipts

For every piece of paper [illegible] parchment [illegible] upon which fhall be written [illegible] any Receipt Difcharge or Acquittance for money amounting to
2l and [illegible] 20l.—Twopence
Amounting to 20l and [illegible] 50l —Fourpence
Amounting to 50l and upwards—Sixpence

To be paid by the perfon by whom fuch Receipts fhall be required.

Exemptions from the above Duties

In all falaries, penfions, debts, or other fums payable from the Crown, the duty fhall be paid by the perfon giving fuch Receipts. Nothing in this act, fhall extend to any Receipt for any legacy, or fhare of a perfonal eftate, or to any Receipt given by the Treafurer of the Navy, for money received for the service of the Navy, or to the Receipt of any agent for money imprested to him on account of the pay of the [illegible] or Ordnance, or to any Receipt by any officer, seaman or soldier, for wages, pay or pension, due from the Navy, Army, or Ordnance; nor to any Receipt to be given for the consideration of the purchase of any share in any public stock or fund, or in the stocks of the Bank, East India, or South-Sea companies, or for the dividends thereof; or to any Receipt given for money deposited in the Banks of England or Scotland, or in the house of any banker [illegible] land, or in the house of any banker [illegible] Receipt on the back of any bill of [illegible] or other note, nor to any release [illegible]

Nor shall the act extend to any Receipt to be given upon any bill or note of the Bank of England, or to any letter acknowledging the Receipt of any [illegible] bills or securities for money, or to any Receipt [illegible] the consideration [illegible] or in any deed, [illegible] nor to any Receipt for draw-backs [illegible] nor to any certificates of [illegible] Customs.

New regulations respecting Receipts.

The full sum and the true date shall be inserted, and all notes, memorandums or writings, whereby any money shall be acknowledged to have been paid, settled, received, accounted for, discharged, released, or in any manner satisfied, or which shall in any manner signify such acknowledgement, and whether the same shall or shall not be signed, shall be deemed a Receipt, and liable to the duties.

Every receipt, note, memorandum, or writing which shall express any general acknowledgement of any debt, claim, account or demand, being paid, settled, received, accounted for, balanced, discharged, released or satisfied, or whereby any [illegible] shall be acknowledged to be in full, and whether signed or not, shall be deemed a Receipt for 20l. and be liable to the duty of sixpence, and no such Receipt, [illegible] shall be available in law or equity, or any other means than [illegible] unless the fine shall be [illegible]

[illegible]

[illegible] be found [illegible] publish, the same [illegible]

[illegible]

[illegible] ceipts.

[illegible]

[illegible] ed may appeal to the Quarter Sessions.—The Justice may mitigate penalties, not less than one moiety be-

[illegible] to attend the [illegible] [illegible] duties [illegible] the whole [illegible] Commissioners of Stamps at their [illegible]

(By [illegible])

[illegible] perform [illegible], a [illegible]

[illegible] —[illegible] shillings
[illegible] —[illegible] shillings
[illegible] —Forty shillings
And every additional - 100l — Twenty [illegible]

*[illegible] the [illegible]

(By [illegible])

If [illegible] receipt is for [illegible] —[illegible] shillings.
[illegible] shillings.
[illegible] grand-
[illegible] for items
[illegible] and [illegible] pence
[illegible]
[illegible] —[illegible] shillings

BEER AND ALE

STRONG [illegible] the Bar[illegible] exclusive of [illegible] Small [illegible] exclusive of [illegible] (a Drink peculiar to Scotland,) a [illegible] D [illegible] mentioned and described in the Seventh Article of the Treaty of Union, 3s. 4d. one hundred and thirteen-four hundred and nineteenths per Barrel.

Beer Imported.

French Beer, Ale or Mum, which shall be imported into Great Britain directly from any of the European Dominions, before landing (by 2. Geo. III. c. 31.) the Barrel to be computed at 30 Gallons Ale Measure, 8l. per Barrel.

Beer, Ale, (including Spruce or Black Beer,) and Mum, other than French, imported from beyond Seas into Great Britain, to be paid before landing thereof, 17s. 3d. per Barrel.

By Annual Malt Act, Mum, imported from France, or any other Country, over and above the Duties last mentioned, is chargeable with 10s. per Barrel.

BRICKS AND TILES.

BRICKS, 5s. 6d. per thousand.

Plain Tiles, 3s. per thousand.

Pan or Ridge Tiles, 8s. per thousand.

Paving Tiles not exceeding 10 Inches Square, 1s. 6d. per hundred.

Ditto exceeding 10 Inches Square, 3s. per hundred.

All other Tiles, 3s. per thousand.

Note. Ten Bricks or Tiles in every hundred to be allowed by the Officer for waste.

CANDLES.

Candles of Tallow, and all other Candles whatsoever (except Wax and Spermaceti Candles) one penny halfpenny per pound.

Candles of Wax or Spermaceti, or which are usually sold either for Wax or Spermaceti Candles, notwithstanding the mixture of any other Ingredients therewith, three pence halfpenny per pound.

Note, Small Rush Lights only once dipped in or drawn through Grease or Kitchen Stuff, and not at all through Tallow melted or refined, and so made by Persons for their own private use, are free of Duty.

Duties on Candles to be paid weekly.

Licences.

By 24 Geo. III c. 36 and 27 Geo. III c. 31 Licences are required to be taken out and paid for annually by the Makers and Retailers of Wax and Spermaceti Candles, viz.

By Makers of Wax and Spermaceti Candles 5l. 15s. each.

By Retailers of Ditto [illegible].

By Chandlers or Makers of Candles other than Wax or Spermaceti Candles, 1l.

*** All Stationers and other Shopkeepers who sell Small Wax Tapers are subject to the Retailers Licence.

Excise Duty on

COCOA NUTS AND COFFEE.

COCOA Nuts, of the Growth or Produce of any British Colony or Plantation in America, imported into Great Britain, and which shall be delivered out of the Warehouse in which the same shall have been lodged under the care and custody of the proper Officers for securing the Duties payable thereon for Home Consumption, sixpence halfpenny per pound.

Cocoa Nuts of the Growth and Produce of any other place, imported and warehoused as above, 1s. 8d. per pound.

Coffee of the Growth or Produce of any British Colony or Plantation in America, imported and warehoused as above, 6d. halfpenny per pound.

Coffee of the Growth or Produce of any other place imported and warehoused as above, 1s. 8d. per pound.

Coffee Roasted.

By 27 Geo. III c. 31 Coffee to be roasted at the Roasting houses provided by the Commissioners, in which any person may send (with a Permit) Coffee Berries to be roasted, and none to be elsewhere roasted ... or ... for sale, by the dealers where there is such a Roasting house 3 three-sevenths per pound with 15l per cent thereon, or 8s per Cwt and 15l per cent

By Dealers when sending their own Roasters ... two-sevenths per pound with 15l per cent thereon, or 3s per Cwt and 15l per cent

CYDER AND PERRY

CYDER or Perry made and sold by Retail, to be paid by the Retailer ... per hogshead

By ... act, Cyder or Perry made and sold by retail, over and above the Duty last mentioned to pay by the respective first Buyers or Retailers ... per hogshead

Cyder or Perry made and sold in Quantities of ... Gallons or upwards, by any Dealer ... or Retailer of Cyder or Perry of the Growth of such Dealer or Retailer to be paid by him, 6s ... per hogshead

Cyder or Perry, of the kind last mentioned, which shall be received into the custody or possession of any Person to be by him sold or disposed of, to be paid by him, 7s. 8d per hogshead

Cyder or Perry consigned to any Factor or Agent who shall receive the same to sell or dispose of, to be paid by such Factor or agent ... 2d per hogshead

Cyder or Perry imported from beyond Seas into Great Britain to be paid by the Importer before landing thereof, ... 16s. 6d per ton

GLASS

OF the Materials or Metal or other preparations whatsoever and by whatever name now or hereafter called used in making of

All Plate, Flint, Enamel, Stained, or Paste Glass, and all Phial Glass whether Apothecary or other Phials, 1l. 1s 5d halfpenny per Cwt.

All spread window Glass, commonly called *Broad Glass*, [illegible] and one half-penny per Cwt.

[illegible] other window Glass, (not being spread Glass,) whether flatted or otherwise manufactured, and commonly [illegible] *Crown Glass*, and all Glass [illegible] *German* [illegible] per Cwt.

[illegible] Glass [illegible] other Vessels and [illegible] Lead, Metal, [illegible] per Cwt. [illegible] Glass Plates [illegible] the [illegible] half-penny per Cwt.

[illegible]

[illegible] Geo. III. [illegible] Duties following were granted on *French* [illegible], viz.

All French Plate Glass imported, 1s. 5d. halfpenny per Square Foot.

All French Flint Glass or French Enamel, Stained, or Paste [illegible] *Flint Glass* imported, [illegible] per [illegible].

All [illegible] Spread Window Glass commonly called *Broad Glass* imported [illegible] Cwt.

[illegible] (not being Spread Glass,) whether [illegible] or otherwise [illegible] *Crown* [illegible] imported, [illegible] per Cwt.

All other Plate Glass [illegible] Manufacture, not otherwise particularly rated or described, [illegible] per Cwt. — See *Excise Duties*.

HIDES AND SKINS.

[illegible] (— Geo. III. [illegible])

All Hides of [illegible], Skins of Calves, [illegible], Seals, Sheep, and Lambs, [illegible]

[illegible] with Sumach or otherwise to resemble [illegible] Leather, [illegible] per pound.

[illegible] Skins [illegible] for Roans (being after the nature of Spanish Leather,) [illegible]d. per pound.

For all other Skins, and parts and pieces of Hides and Skins, not particularly rated as above, 30l per cent *ad valorem*.

By 31 Geo. III c. 27, the foregoing duties of Excise on goat and sheep skins are to continue in force until the 5th day of July 1791, when the following duties are to be levied in lieu thereof.

For every dozen of tanned goat skins imported, an additional duty of customs, with drawback on exportation of 15s.

For every dozen of goat skins tanned with simach or otherwise in Great Britain, an Excise duty of 5s.

For every dozen of sheep skins tanned for roans 2s. 3d.

Tawed.

All Hides of Horses, Mares, and Geldings, dressed in Allum and Salt, or Meal, or otherwise tawed, 1s. 6d. per Hide.

All other Hides, 3s. per Hide.

All Calf, Kip, and Seal Skins, 1d. halfpenny per pound.

Slink Calf Skins with the hair on, 3s. per Dozen.

Slink Calf without hair, and all Dog Skins and Kid Skins, (except such Kid Skins as paid the full duty on Importation) 1s. per Dozen.

Buck and Doe Skins, (except such as paid the full duty on Importation) 6d. per pound.

Goat and Beaver Skins, 2s. per Dozen.

Sheep and Lamb Skins, 1d. farthing per pound.

For all other Skins, and parts and pieces of Skins, not particularly rated as above, 30l. per cent *ad valorem*.

Hides and Skins dressed in Oil.

By 28. Geo. III c. [illegible], all Hides and Skins of Buck, Deer, and Elk, 1s. per pound.

By ditto, Sheep and Lamb Skins, 3d. per pound.

By ditto, for all other Skins, and parts and pieces of Skins, not particularly rated as above, 6d. per pound.

Vellum Skins, [illegible]s. 3d. halfpenny per Dozen.

Parchment Skins, 1s. 8d. three farthings per Dozen.

Note. By 24. Geo. III c. 19. no Tanner can be a Butcher, Shoemaker, or Currier. *See Excise Licences.*

HOPS

HOPS cured and made fit for use, one farthing twelve-twentieths, per pound.

DUTIES ON QUACK MEDICINES.

(23 Geo. III. c. 62.)

FOR and upon every packet, box, bottle, phial or other inclosure containing any drugs, oils, waters, essences, tinctures, powders, or other preparation or composition whatsoever used or applied, or to be used or applied externally or internally, as medicines or medicaments for the prevention, cure, or relief of any disorder or complaint incident to, or in any wise affecting the human body, which shall be uttered or vended in Great Britain, there shall be charged a Stamp-duty according to the rates following (that is to say), where the contents of any such packet, box, bottle, phial or other inclosure aforesaid, shall not exceed the price or value of 1s. there shall be charged a Stamp-duty of one penny halfpenny.

Where the contents of any such packet, box, bottle, &c. shall exceed the price of 1s. and not exceed 2s. 6d. there shall be charged a Stamp-duty of 3d.—above 2s. 6d. and under 5s. a Stamp-duty of 6d.—and if of the price of 5s. or upwards a Stamp-duty of 1s.

The above duties not to extend to articles mentioned in two books of rates referred to by 12 Car. II. cap. 4. and 11 Geo. I. cap. 7. nor to unmixed drugs sold by a regular surgeon, apothecary, chemist or druggist, who hath served a regular apprenticeship, or by any person who hath served as a surgeon in the navy or army, nor to preparations sold by regular surgeons, &c. not claiming an exclusive right to the same, and which are not prepared or sold under letters patent, nor by any public notice, or advertisement.

Every person uttering or vending any such drugs, &c. shall annually take out a Licence for that purpose, for which each person shall pay in London, or within the limits of the penny post, 20s and in any other part of the kingdom, 5s

The duties to be under the management of the Commissioners for Stamps, who are to grant licence for one year, from Sept [illegible], or any subsequent day New licences to be taken out ten days before the old expire

Every person making, or vending any such drugs, medicines, &c shall from time to time [illegible] to the Commissioners or to their officers paper covers for [illegible] such packets, &c [illegible] labels, for or their [illegible] the value thereof that the same may be stamped as the Commissioners shall direct and every such packet bottle, &c shall have affixed thereto, such cover stamped, and distinguished as aforesaid.

Penalties

Persons selling articles liable to such duties without a licence, forfeit [illegible]l for each offence

Persons vending articles subject to such duties without a stamp affixed thereto, or with a label stamped of less value than directed forfeit for every offence [illegible]l

Persons using the same label a second time &c forfeit for every offence [illegible]l

Persons selling or having labels for the purpose of being used a second time forfeit for every offence [illegible]l

Either buyer or seller may inform

An allowance of two pounds *per cent* for prompt payment of [illegible]l and [illegible] *per cent* for [illegible]l

Every person who shall prepare or vend any medicines or other articles liable to the duties shall give notice in writing of the usual place where they prepare, or sell the same which notice shall be sent to the Commissioners or to their officers next to the place where such medicines &c shall be prepared or sold, which notice shall contain the true and just name, qualities and prices of each article upon pain of forfeiting for every offence, [illegible]l

The duties hereby imposed shall extend, and be deemed and adjudged to extend to all pills, powders, lozenges, tinctures, potions, cordials, electuaries plasters, unguents salves, ointments, drops, lotions oils spirits, medicated herbs and waters, chemical and official preparations whatsoever of the like properties, prepared, or sold, by any person who hath any secret for the making or preparing the same or any exclusive right, or which hath been sold under the authority of letters patent, or by any public notice or advertisement, or handbills recommended as nostrums or proprietary medicines, or as specifics or otherwise, for the prevention, cure or relief of any disorder malady, ailment, or complaint

MALT

Perpetual Duties

EVERY maker of malt is, under the penalty of 10l to take out a licence annually from the Excise Office according to 24 Geo. III [illegible]

Maltsters, who make not more than 50 quarters annually are to pay for the licence [illegible] who make more than 50 and less than 100 [illegible]—between 100 and 150 [illegible]—Between 150 and 200 [illegible]—between 250 and 300 [illegible]—Between 350 and 400, [illegible]—between 400 and 450 [illegible]—between 500 and 550 2l 15s.—exceeding 550 [illegible]

Maltsters to pay 5s. for a licence besides the duty annually according to the quantity made

Maltsters who withdraw their entries and make fresh ones to pay the whole duty

By 27 Geo. III c. 13 there shall be paid for every bushel of malt, made within *England*, to be paid by the maker 9d. three-fourths.

Within Scotland [illegible] three-fourths and ten twentieth parts of a farthing

For every bushel brought from *Scotland* into *England*, with a certificate from the officer that it hath paid the duty of 4d three-fourths and ten-twentieths, there shall be paid a duty of 5d three-fourths and ten twentieths. But if brought without such certificate, a duty of 9d. three-fourths.

Annual Duty

By 12 Ann, stat 1 c 2 (which act is continued by an annual bill) there shall be paid for every bushel of malt which shall be made within England, Wales, and Berwick, sixpence

Within Scotland three pence, and if brought into England, with certificate that this duty has been paid to pay three pence more, if brought without a certificate, to pay sixpence

Additional temporary Duty, in 1791

By 31 Geo. III. c 2 after 5th January 1791 there shall be paid, above all other duties, for every bushel of malt made within England, Wales and Berwick, three pence.

Within Scotland, one penny halfpenny, and for every bushel brought from thence into England, an additional penny halfpenny

The new duties shall be paid for every bushel of malt belonging to any maltster, seller of malt, brewer, distiller, inn keeper, or vinegar maker either in his own possession or in the possession of any other person in trust for him, upon Jan. 5, 1791 to be paid by the person possessed of such malt, above all other duties, in manner following, viz. one third part on Feb. 5 1791, one-third on March 5, 1791, and the remaining third part on April 5, 1791

Allowance on the perpetual Duty

By 27 Geo. III c 13 for every quarter of malt that shall be made and locked up for exportation, and exported, three pence.

Allowances to the common Brewer.

There shall be paid to every common brewer or persons who brew beer or ale, and tap out or sell the the same publicly or privately

Upon every barrel of beer or ale, above six shillings the barrel, (exclusive of the duties of Excise) brewed by the common brewer, &c. within London and Westminster or the bills of mortality and returned by the gauger By 27 Geo. III c. 13. 1s. 4d By 31 Geo. III c. 2. 8d.—Total 2s.

And without the bills of mortality, by 27 Geo. III. c 13 1s. 8d By 31 Geo. III c. 2 10d. Total 2s 6d

Beer or ale, of six shillings the barrel or under, brewed throughout England, Wales, and Berwick By 27 Geo. III. c. 13. 4d By 31 Geo. III. c 2 2d Tot. 6d.

Beer or ale above six shillings the barrel, and not exceeding eleven shillings, commonly called Table Beer, brewed within London, Westminster, or the bills of mortality By 31 Geo. III. c. 2. 1d

And without the bills of mortality, by 31 Geo. III c 2 3d farthing

Beer or ale above six shillings the barrel, brewed within Scotland. By 27 Geo. III c 13 10d By 31 Geo. III c 2 5d. Total, 1s. 3d

Upon every barrel of two penny ale, in Article VII. of the Union brewed within Scotland By 27 Geo III c 13 6d By 31 Geo. III c 2 3d. Total, 9d

Upon every barrel of six shillings beer or ale, brewed within Scotland. By 27 Geo. III c. 13. 3d. By 31 Geo. III c 2. 1d halfpenny Tot. 4d halfpenny

Which allowances are to be paid at the end of four months after the duties have been paid, 20 Geo. III c 35, and 31 Geo. III c. 2

If any common brewer, &c. shall after the end of 4 months, leave with the Collector of Excise of the district, and where the duties were paid a certificate from the Officer who received the duties, That the duties upon beer or ale have been paid (which certificate the Officer is to give gratis) then the Collector shall out of the duties on malt, forthwith pay the person producing the certificate the allowances direct-

ed, and in case the Collector shall not have money in hand to pay, then the Commissioners of Excise are to pay the allowances out of the duties on malt, or any monies then in their hands, 20 Geo. III c. [illegible] and 21 Geo. III c. 2.

By 21 Geo. III c. 2 the new duties are to be paid into the Exchequer, and kept separate from other monies. And all monies arising thereon before April 5, 1792, shall be carried to the consolidated fund, and after April 5, 1792 shall, together with such other duties as shall be granted by any act of this session, be a fund for payment of 800,000l. part of 1,800,000l. to be raised by loans or Exchequer bills by [illegible] act of this session, together with interest on the said 800,000l. and shall be applied towards paying off the 800,000l. and interest, and no other purpose.

On payment of the 800,000l. and interest the new duties on malt, and additional allowances, are to cease.

SPIRITUOUS LIQUORS.

Foreign Spirits.

DEALERS in brandy are to take out an Excise licence annually, and pay 5l. for the same, by 24 Geo. III c. 41 on penalty of 50l.

Foreign Spirits are subject to the following duties, payable at the Custom-house on importation.

	Duty.	Drawb.
Arrack imported by the East India company, brandy, and geneva, per gallon - - -	L.0 0 0	0 0 8
Citron water, the gallon -	0 5 8	0 5 1
Hungary water, [illegible], Usquebaugh, cordial water, strong water, and all spirits not enumerated, the gallon, - -	0 2 10	0 2 7
Rum British, the gallon, - -	0 0 5	0 0 3
Foreign, - - -	0 0 7	0 0 6

And there is moreover to be paid for brandy rum, spirits, or aquavitae, imported into Great Britain, the duties of Excise following, to be paid by the importer, before the landing thereof

		Total Duty.
Old Duty.	For every gallon of single brandy, by 27 Geo. III. c. 13. 4s. 3d.	0 5 1
New Duty	By 31 Geo. III. c. 1 10d.	
Old.	For every gallon above proof, by 27 Geo III c. 13 8s. 1d.	0 9 9
New.	By 31 Geo. III c. 1 1s. 8d.	
Old	For every gallon of rum spirits, or aquavitae, of the produce of the British plantations, 27 Geo III. c. 13 3s 7d.	0 4 3
New	By 31 Geo. III c. 1 8d.	
Old	For every gallon above proof, by 27 Geo. III c. 13 6s. 8d.	0 8 0
New	By 31 Geo. III. c. 1 1s. 4d.	

For every gallon of such rum, &c. in any warehouse, on Dec 28, 1790, and delivered out after that day, 8d. and for every gallon above proof so delivered 1s. 4d. to be paid by the importer, upon demand. 31 Geo. III c. 1

		Total Duty
Old	For every gallon of single spirits or aquavitae (other than such brandy, rum, &c. as aforesaid) by 27 Geo. III. c. 13. 4s. 3d.	0 5 1
New	By 31 Geo. III. c. 1 10d.	
Old	For every gallon above proof, by 27 Geo. III c. 13. 8s. 1d	0 9 9
New	By 31 Geo. III c 1 1s. 8d.	

The additional duties on rum may be bonded in the same manner as the old duties, and a drawback of the additional duty shall also be allowed for all such rum, &c. of the British plantations, on the shipping thereof as stores. 31 Geo. III. c. 1

British Spirits

Distillers and Rectifiers are, the Corn Distiller under the penalty of 200l. and Molasses Distiller and Rectifiers under the penalty of [illegible]l. to take out an Excise licence annually, paying one shilling per [illegible] *per* gallon for the contents of their stills. 24 Geo. III c. [illegible]

And there shall be paid by them over the duties of Excise following:

		L. s. D.
Old	For every gallon of fermented wort or wash, made in England for extracting spirits for home consumption, from any malt, corn, grain, or malts, or any mixture with the same, by 27 Geo. III c. 13. 6d	
New	By 31 Geo. III c. 1 [illegible]d	0 0 7
Old	—— of cyder or perry, or any other liquor brewed in England, for extracting spirits for home consumption, by 27 Geo. III c. 13. 5d	
New	By 31 Geo. III c. [illegible] [illegible]d	0 0 6
Old	—— from molasses or sugar, by 27 Geo. III c. [illegible] [illegible]d [illegible]	
New	By 31 Geo. III c. 1 [illegible] half-penny	0 0 [illegible]
Old	—— from foreign refined [illegible] wine, or foreign cyder, or wash prepared from foreign materials except molasses and sugar, [illegible] Geo. III c. [illegible]	
New	By 31 Geo. III c. 1 2d	0 1 2

SCOTS LOWLAND DISTILLERY LICENCE

BY 26 Geo. III c. [illegible] the Excise rates and duties [illegible] [illegible] former [illegible] of Parliament upon low wines and spirits and worts or wash in Scotland (except in the Highland counties) are discontinued for one year, to be computed from the 5th July 1788, and by 29 Geo III c 14 sect 7, the said act (of 28 Geo III) is revived and continued in force from 5th July 1789 to the 5th July 1790, and continued by 31 Geo III

The several rates and duties after mentioned, during the space of one year, are to be charged and paid by way of annual licences, in lieu and instead of all former duties, &c

On stills where grain or other British materials are used

For every gallon of wine measure of the content of each still, including the head thereof used for making low wines and spirits from corn, grain, malt, tilts, cyder, or perry, or other wash or liquor made from British materials, or any mixture therewith, the yearly sum of 3l per gallon

On stills where molasses are used

For every gallon wine measure of the content of each still including the head thereof, used for making of low wines and spirits from molasses or sugar, or any mixture therewith, the yearly sum of 3s per gallon

On stills where foreign materials are used

For every gallon wine measure of the content of each still including the head thereof, used for making of low wines or spirits from foreign refused wine, or foreign cyder, or wash prepared from foreign materials, or any mixture therewith, the yearly sum of 6l per gallon

Provided always, That no wash still licenced, as above mentioned, shall be under 100 gallons content including the head thereof, and that there be at the same time also licenced a doubling still of 1 4th, the content of the wash still

By sect 36, Distillers who shall make spirits for exportation to England, to make entry in writing of their intention four days at least before they begin their operations, in terms prescribed by this act, and on removing of spirits from any warehouse to be rectified or compounded, an allowance is to be made to them of two gallons in every hundred for evaporation; if any deficiency shall appear in the spirits so taken or not properly accounted for, the distiller to be charged a duty of 5s. per gallon

By sect. [illegible], Distillers for exportation of spirits to England, are to be allowed a proportional abatement of the excise duty paid by them in the following manner, viz.

For every [illegible] contents of stills used for making spirits for exportation to England,

If from grain, or any other British materials for every gallon of the contents, [illegible] 4 [illegible]

If from molasses or sugar, or any mixture therewith, 4 [illegible]

If from foreign materials [illegible]

By sect. [illegible], Distillers of spirits for exportation to England, to produce to the officer the following quantities of spirits for every 100 gallons of wash, viz.

For every 100 gallons of wash from grain, or any other British materials, 15 and one [illegible] gallons of spirits of the strength of 1 to 10 over hydrometer proof.

For every 100 gallons of wash from molasses or sugar, or any mixture therewith, 18 and one half gallons of spirits of the strength of 1 to 10 over hydrometer proof.

For every 100 gallons of wash from foreign materials, 10 and one half gallons of spirits of the strength of 1 to 10 over hydrometer proof.

And if the [illegible] spirits extracted by any distiller fall short of the above proportions, the duties following to be paid [illegible]

For every [illegible] gallon of spirits from

Grain or any other British materials 2s. 9[illegible] and by 31 Geo. III. c. [illegible] an additional duty of [illegible] half penny. In whole [illegible] half [illegible] per gallon.

Molasses, or sugar or any mixture therewith, 2s. 10d. halfpenny per gallon

Foreign materials, 5s per gallon

For every gallon of such spirits of superior strength than 1 to 10 over proof, and not exceeding [illegible] per [illegible] 1 to 10 over proof, an additional duty in proportion to the surplus strength, to be paid by the importer before landing 27 Geo III c 13 and 31 Geo III c 1

SCOTS HIGHLAND DISTILLERY LICENCES

BY 2[illegible] Geo III c 22 annual licences may be granted by the Commissioners of Excise to [illegible] authorise persons qualified as this law directs within the several counties of Orkney, Caithness, Sutherland, Ross, Cromarty, Inverness, Argyle, Bute, Stirling, Clackmannan, Perth, Dumbarton, Aberdeen, Forfar, Kincardine, Banff, Nairn, and Elgin, to erect and keep stills the cubical contents whereof shall not be less than 2[illegible] nor more than [illegible]0 gallons including their respective heads, on payment of the sum of 20s for each gallon of such still, [illegible] per gallon

This licence shall be in place of both the distillery and malt duties imposed by former acts, and shall be allowed and considered only as a composition at the rate of [illegible] bolls of malt, and [illegible]600 gallons of spirits produced by a still of [illegible] gallons and the like proportion shall be observed both as to the quantity of malt and spirits, when a licence shall be taken out for any still of a less size.—Excise officers may enter and survey malt-barns and distilleries, and charge with the usual duty all malt and spirits exceeding these quantities

Note No stills to be licensed in the counties of Dumbarton, Stirling, Clackmannan, and Perth, agreeable to the boundaries directed by this act

By the above act, for every gallon contents over [illegible] and above the dimensions of a still, for which a licence is taken out, a further duty of [illegible] per gallon

Note, If such surplus shall exceed three English gallons, the still and utensils together with the licence, to be forfeited, and the distiller liable for a penalty of 20l Sterling.

LICENCES TO ALE-HOUSE-KEEPERS, &c.

Duties upon Licences for retailing Wines, Sweets, and distilled Spirituous Liquors (30 Geo III c. 38.)

AFTER October 10, 1790, all persons who shall retail foreign wines, or British made wines, or sweets, or distilled spirituous liquors, or strong waters, shall before they retail any of the above articles, take out such licences hereafter mentioned as the case may require, which licence shall be granted in the following manner

If any such licence be granted within the chief office of Excise in London, the same shall be granted under the hands and seals of two or more commissioners of Excise in England, or by such persons as they shall appoint, but if the licence shall be taken out in any part of the kingdom not within the said limits, they shall be granted under the hands and seals of the collectors and supervisors of Excise within their respective districts, and in Scotland in the same manner, upon paying the several sums of money following

	£	s	d
To retail foreign wine in England if the party has not a spirit or beer licence,	5	4	0
If the party has a beer licence and not one for spirits, - - - - -	4	4	0
If the party has also a spirit licence, -	2	4	0
For every licence to retail British made wines or sweets, either in England or Scotland	2	4	0
To retail foreign wines in Scotland if the party has not a spirit or beer licence, -	3	6	8
If he has a beer licence, but not one for spirits, - - - - -	2	13	4
If he has also a spirit licence, -	1	6	8

For every licence to retail spirits in Great

	£	s.	d.
Britain, if the party's house be rated under 15 pounds per annum, - -	4	14	0
If at 15 and under 20 - -	5	2	0
If at 20 and under 25 - - - -	5	10	0
If at 25 and under 30 - - -	5	18	0
If at 30 and under 40 - - - - -	6	6	0
If at 40 and under 50 - - - - -	6	14	0
If at 50 or upwards - - - - -	7	2	0

These licences to be renewed annually; every person who sells foreign wine retail without a licence, or renewing it in time, forfeits 50l.

On death or removal, upon application to the commissioners or collectors, or supervisors, as before recited, the executors, &c. will be authorised to carry on the trade for the remainder of the term.

One licence is sufficient for a partnership in one house.

A licence is not to authorise the sale of wine, &c. in any other house than that for which it was granted.

No persons are to have licences granted them but such as might have licences before the passing of this bill.

The two Universities, the Vintners Company in London, and the Corporation of Saint Alban's, are not to be injured by this bill.

All persons shall be deemed retailers of foreign wine who sell it in any less quantity than shall be equal to the measure or quantity in which it may have been lawfully imported by way of merchandise.

Any person selling 25 gallons or under of British made wine or sweets is deemed a retailer of that article.

All persons who shall sell brandy, rum, arrack, usquebaugh, geneva, aquavitae, or any other distilled spirituous liquor or strong water, unmixed or mixed, in any less quantity than two gallons, shall be deemed a retailer of spirituous liquors.

From the before-mentioned 10th day of October, 1790, the several acts made in the 9th of Queen Anne, 30 and 31 of Geo. II. and 26 of Geo. III. as far as they authorise the commissioners of stamps to grant licences, and the 16th and 2[illegible]th of Geo. II. and the 27th of Geo. III. as far as they authorise the commissioners of excise to grant licences, are repealed.

The powers of former acts relating to the [illegible] of wines, &c. (unless hereby altered) to continue in full force.

The powers of the 12th of Car. II. c. 24, or any other act relating to excise, are to extend to this act.

N. B. By 2[illegible]th Geo. III. c. 2[illegible], no person shall by virtue of such licence be permitted to sell British made wines or sweets, for consumption in his own house, unless he shall also have obtained an ale licence.

GOLD AND SILVER PLATE LICENCES

BY 31 Geo. II. c. 32, and 28 Geo. III. c. 37, by every seller of or dealer in gold or silver plate, or goods or wares containing above 2 dwts. and less than 2 oz. of gold, or above 5 dwts. and less than 30 oz. of silver, to be paid per advance, [illegible]l. 6s. each.

By 32 Geo. II. c. [illegible] and 28 Geo. III. c. 37, by every seller of, or dealer in gold or silver in any one piece containing 2 oz. or upwards of gold, or 30 oz. and upwards of silver, and by every pawnbroker trading in or selling any gold or silver plate, or any goods or wares whereon any gold or silver is manufactured, and by every refiner of gold and silver, to be paid as above, 5l. 15s. each.

DUTY ON GOLD AND SILVER PLATE

UPON all gold plate which shall be imported into the kingdom of Great Britain, or which shall be made within the said kingdom, a duty after the rate of [illegible]s. for every ounce.

Upon all silver plate which shall be imported into the kingdom of Great Britain, or which shall be made within the said kingdom, a duty after the rate of 6d. for every ounce.

EXCISE LICENCES

BY 21 Geo. III licences are required to be taken out by the makers of, and dealers in [illegible] Excisable Commodities, and certain duties [illegible] to be paid per annum [illegible] by the following persons, *viz.*

By makers of mead for sale, 1l.

makers of any kind of sweets (except mead for sale) 5l.

makers of vinegar for sale, 10l.

Soap-makers 2l.

Paper-stainers and paper-makers, 2l.

Callicoe printers and printers, painters, or stainers of silks, linens, cottons, or stuffs 10l.

Starch-makers 5l.

Wire-drawers [illegible]

Tanners living within the bills of mortality, 5l.

All others, 2l. 10l.

Tawers, 1l.

Dressers of hides and skins in oil 2l.

Curriers 2l.

Makers of vellum or parchment 1l.

Glass-makers, for every glass-house, 10l.

Penalties.

From 10th September 1781, no person to make any of the aforesaid commodities, without first having obtained a licence.

Licences shall be granted under the hands and seals of two or more Commissioners of Excise, and these licences to be renewed annually.

Persons acting without a licence subject to the penalties following: [illegible] vinegar-makers, callicoe printers, and starch makers, 50l.

Soap-makers, paper-stainers, wire-drawers, dressers of hides and curriers, 20l.

Makers of mead, tanners, and vellum and parchment makers, [illegible]

These duties to be under the management of the Commissioners of Excise.

And persons in partnership need take but one licence for one house.

PRINTED GOODS

PAPER Printed, Painted or Stained [illegible] hangings [illegible] other uses [illegible] above the Duties [illegible] are [illegible] farthing per yard [illegible]

All calicoes, muslins, linens, stuffs and [illegible] under mentioned [illegible] except such as [illegible] and [illegible] of woollen, or whereof the [illegible] shall be woollen shall pay the duties following [illegible]

[illegible] muslins printed in [illegible] and all French printed calicoes and muslins [illegible] ported directly from any of the Europe [illegible] dominions of the French King, [illegible] per yard square

Linens and stuffs made either of cotton or linen mixed with other materials, fustians, velvets, velverets, dimities and other figured [illegible], made of cotton and other materials mixed [illegible] of cotton wool, wove and printed in Great Britain. The like linens and stuffs [illegible] French printed, imported directly from any of the [illegible] dominions of the French King. Stuffs wholly made of cotton wool [illegible] and proved [illegible] by having [illegible] thread in each [illegible] commonly called British Manufactory and [illegible] printed muslins. And by [illegible] Geo. III c [illegible] all [illegible] printed linens and stuffs [illegible] enumerated above, [illegible] per yard square

Silks [illegible] and [illegible] duties payable [illegible] import [illegible] yard [illegible] and three [illegible]

Silk [illegible] above the duties payable at importation [illegible] per yard square

By [illegible] boards [illegible] less than [illegible] are to be charged [illegible] only

TEA.

ON the gross price of tea, as sold at the sales of the East India Company, to be paid by the purchaser to the Company, and by them to the commissioners of Excise, [illegible] per cent. Excise duty.

By 20 Geo. III. c. 35, and 28 Geo. III. c. [illegible] every dealer in coffee, [illegible] and chocolate, [illegible] must take out a licence annually, for which he shall pay [illegible] 5s 6d.

SOAP.

HARD cake or ball soap, [illegible] farthings per pound. Soft soap, [illegible] three farthings per pound.

By [illegible] Geo. III. c. [illegible] duties on soap to be paid weekly. (See Excise Licences.)

STARCH.

STARCH of what kind soever, [illegible] farthing per pound. By [illegible] Geo. III. c. 8 [illegible] starch maker, must be painted over the door, or on the front of the store-house and no starch [illegible] pounds, shall be removed, unless the word STARCH, be legibly marked on the package. (See Excise Licences.)

SWEETS.

ALL liquors made for sale, from fruit or sugar, or any mixture therewith, commonly called sweets or made wines, 1s 4d three farthings per barrel. (See Excise Licences.)

VERJUICE.

VERJUICE made for sale, 7s 8d per hogshead.

VINEGAR

VINEGAR, vinegar-beer or liquors prepared for vinegar made for sale, 10s. and three farthings per barrel. (See Excise Licences.)

DOGS

BY 10. Geo. III. c. 18. persons stealing dogs from the owners, or persons intrusted therewith, or selling, buying, receiving, or retaining dogs, knowing the same to be stolen, and convicted on the oath of one witness before two justices, shall pay not more than 30l. nor less than 20l. for the first offence, with charges, and on non-payment may be committed for twelve months, and not less than six.

For the second offence to pay 50l. and not less than 30l. with charges, one moiety to the informer, and the other to the poor; and on non-payment may be committed for eighteen months, and not less than twelve, and to be publickly whipped in three days [illegible].

Search may be made for dogs and skins stolen, and the persons in whose custody found liable to the same penalties. Appeal lies to the quarter sessions, where costs may be given, but no certiorari.

FISH

(5 Geo. III. c. 14.)

ALL persons entering any park, paddock, garden, orchard, or yard, inclosed, belonging to any dwelling-house, in which there is any river or any other water, and shall by any device whatsoever, take fish from thence without the permission of the owner, or shall buy or receive such fish, knowing it to be so taken, shall be transported for seven years.

Any persons committing the above offence, where

the pond, river, &c. is not inclosed, yet is private property, for its [illegible]

Upon oath being made by one or more credible witnesses of the offence, any Justice of Peace may issue his warrant to bring the offender before him, and order the penalty to be immediately paid upon conviction, or be committed for six months.

LIMITATIONS, STATUTES OF,

within which Actions must be brought.

BY 21 Jac. I. c. 2, concealed lands shall not be recovered by the King, unless the profits have been [illegible] within sixty years before this parliament, or have stood in *super* of record. [illegible] this is not [illegible] the duty of 2d [illegible] at Newcastle.

All writs of formedon shall be sued, and entry [illegible] made within twenty years after the title and cause of action [illegible] 21 Jac. c. 16.

Infants, femes covert, persons [illegible] or [illegible] shall bring [illegible] enter within ten years after disability removed. *Ibid.*

Actions [illegible] other than between merchant and merchant, trespass, debt, detinue, trover and [illegible] brought within six years after cause [illegible] action set after within four years, and of slander within two years. *Ibid.*

On writ of judgment, or outlawry for error, the plaintiff may commence a new action within a year. *Ibid.*

Where the trespass on lands is involuntary, the defendant may plead a disclaimer of any title thereto, and a tender of amends before action brought. *Ibid.*

Persons disabled [illegible] or otherwise when cause of action accrued, may bring the same action within the same time after disability removed. *Ibid.*

By 10 and 11 W. III. c. 14 no fine, recovery, or judgment shall be reversed unless writ of error be brought w[illegible] twenty years after [illegible], but perſons diſabled by [illegible] or otherwiſe, ſhall bring ſuch writ of error within five years after the diſability removed.

By 4 Ann c 16, no claim or entry ſhall be of force to avoid a fine with proclamations, unleſs an action be commenced within a year after ſuch entry.

Suits for ſeamen's wages in the Admiralty ſhall be commenced within ſix years after the cauſe of action accrued. *Ib.*

Such cauſe of action falling to one diſabled by infancy or otherwiſe, may be purſued within ſix years after the diſability removed. *Ibid.*

[illegible] perſons gone beyond the ſeas, may be brought within the times limited after their return. *Ibid.*

ADDITIONAL TEMPORARY DUTY OF TEN PER CENT

BY 3[illegible] Geo III there ſhall be paid upon every aſſeſſment to be made after April 5, 1791, for or in reſpect of the ſeveral duties under the management of the [illegible] of taxes, an additional duty after the rate of 10 per cent upon the groſs amount of all the former duties charged by ſuch aſſeſſment.

And there ſhall be paid upon every aſſeſſment made for the year ending April 5, 1791, an additional duty of 10l per cent upon the groſs amount of all the [illegible] duties charged by ſuch aſſeſſment, to be computed for the half year ending 5 April 1791.

But this additional duty is not to be charged on the amount of the Land Tax, nor on the [illegible] of the new duties on windows, impoſed by 24 Geo III c 38 (commonly called the Commutation Act.)

The new duties are to be charged in addition to the duties on houſes, on the old window Tax, on windows, &c on horſes, on ſervants, and on coaches, &c.

The additional duty for the half year ending April 5, 1791, ſhall be paid by equal portions on Jan 5, and April 5, [illegible]

[illegible] April [illegible], 1791, the additional duties [illegible] to be paid quarterly.

N. B. The former duties are also payable quarterly, though collected half yearly.

The additional duties shall be paid into the Exchequer, and kept [illegible] from [illegible] and all [illegible] before April [illegible] 2 [illegible] to the consolidated fund [illegible] with [illegible] to the payment of [illegible] and interest [illegible] Exchequer bills [illegible] of the [illegible] interest [illegible] additional duty shall cease.

PAWNBROKERS LICENCES

(2[illegible] Geo. III [illegible])

FROM [illegible] July, 178[illegible], every pawnbroker [illegible] Westminster, the Borough of Southwark [illegible] St [illegible] St Pancras, [illegible] bills of mortality shall take out a licence [illegible] they shall pay a stamp duty of [illegible]

Pawnbrokers residing in any other part of the kingdom [illegible]

[illegible] their licences to the [illegible] in the country.

Every pawnbroker [illegible] licence forfeits [illegible] renewed [illegible] days [illegible] months from the [illegible] the former [illegible]

[illegible] goods or chattels for the re[illegible] shall be deemed a pawnbroker [illegible]

[illegible] money [illegible] upon goods and chattels [illegible] red [illegible] pawnbrokers [illegible]

[illegible] partnership, whether [illegible] two or more [illegible] concerned, but every [illegible] shop where the business of taking in pawns is carried on must have a separate licence.

Counterfeiting stamps on licences is by this act a capital offence.

An Act for further regulating the trade or business of Pawnbrokers.

PAWNBROKERS by this act may legally take a profit after the following rates:

For every pledge upon which there shall have been lent any sum not exceeding two shillings and sixpence, one halfpenny, for any time the said pledge shall remain in pawn, not exceeding one calendar month, and the like for every month afterwards, including the month in which such pledge shall be redeemed, although such month shall not be expired.

Where there shall have been lent five shillings, one penny.

Where there shall have been lent seven shillings and sixpence, one penny halfpenny.

Where there shall have been lent ten shillings, two pence.

Where there shall have been lent twelve shillings and sixpence, two pence halfpenny.

Where there shall have been lent fifteen shillings, three pence.

Where there shall have been lent seventeen shillings and sixpence, three pence halfpenny.

Where there shall have been lent one pound, four-pence, and so on progressively and in proportion for any sum not exceeding forty shillings.

Where there shall have been lent any sum above forty shillings, and not exceeding ten pounds, at and after the rate of three pence and no more, for the loan of every twenty shillings, by the calendar month including the current month, and so in proportion for any fractional sum.

Which sums shall be taken as a full satisfaction for interest and warehouse room.

When goods are pawned for any sum of money exceeding five shillings, the pawnbroker before he advances the money shall enter, in a fair and regular manner, in a book kept by him for that purpose, a description of the goods or chattels which he shall receive in pawn, the sum of money to be advanced thereon, with the day of the month and year on which, and the name and place of abode of the person by whom such goods are so pawned, and also the name and place of abode of the owner thereof, according to the information of the person pawning the same, and where the money lent on any goods shall not exceed the sum of five shillings entry shall be made in the book by the pawnbroker within four hours after the said goods shall have been so pawned, and every pawnbroker shall, at the time of taking every pawn whatsoever, give to the person so pawning the same, a note fairly written or printed, or in part written and in part printed, containing therein a description of the goods which he shall receive in pawn, and also the sum advanced with the day and the name and place of abode of the person by whom such goods are so pawned, and the name and place of abode of the owner thereof, also upon the said note, or on the back thereof, shall be written or printed the name and place of abode of the pawnbroker giving the same; which said note, the party pawning the said goods is required to accept in all cases, and the pawnbroker shall not receive such pledge unless the party pledging shall accept the same and every such note where the sum lent shall be less than five shillings, shall be delivered gratis if five shillings and less than ten shillings the pawnbroker may take one halfpenny for the same, if ten shillings, and less than twenty shillings one penny if twenty shillings, and less than five pounds, two pence if five pounds, or upwards four pence, and no more and which note shall be produced to the pawnbroker before he shall be obliged to re-deliver the respective goods, except as hereinafter is excepted

Persons pawning goods are allowed seven days after the expiration of the first month without paying any thing for the said seven days, and if, after the expiration of seven days, and before the expiration of fourteen days, by paying for one month and a half,

I

but if the fourteen days have expired, the pawnbroker is intitled to the interest of the second month, and the same regulation takes place in every subsequent month.

Persons pawning goods the property of others, shall upon conviction before a justice or justices of the peace forfeit the sum of twenty shillings, together with the value of the goods so pawned, and in case of non-payment of the forfeiture, to be committed to the house of correction, and to be kept to hard labour for no less time than one callendar month, nor longer than three, unless the forfeit shall be sooner paid, and within three days before the expiration of the said term shall be publickly whipped, and the said forfeitures, when recovered, shall be applied towards making satisfaction to the party injured, and defraying the costs of the prosecution, as shall be considered reasonable by the justice; but if the party injured declines to accept of such satisfaction and costs, or if there should be any overplus of the said forfeitures, after making and paying the same, the forfeitures or the overplus shall be applied to the use of the poor of the parish where such offence shall have been committed.

Persons forging or counterfeiting notes, or procuring them to be done, or selling them knowing them to be forged, it shall be lawful for any person who shall have reason to suspect the same, to seize and detain such person uttering or offering the forged note, and to deliver him into the custody of a constable, who shall convey such person to some justice of the peace where the offence shall have been committed; and upon conviction the party shall be committed to the common goal or house of correction there to be imprisoned for any time not exceeding three calendar months, nor less than one, at the discretion of such justice.

Persons bringing goods to pawn, not giving a good account of themselves, or refusing to give an account at all, or upon suspicion of offering stolen goods, or any person not intitled to redeem goods in pawn, shall endeavour to redeem the same, it shall be lawful for any person, or his agent, to whom such goods are so offered, or with whom such goods are so pledged to seize and deliver such person into the custody of a constable who shall carry him before a justice of the peace where the offence is committed, and should there appear any ground of the said offences, after a second examination they shall be committed to the common goal or house of correction where the offence shall be committed, there to be dealt with according to law, but where the nature of the offence shall not authorize such proceedings they shall be committed for any time not exceeding three calendar months, nor less than one, at the discretion of such justice.

Goods unlawfully pawned without the privity of the owner, any justice of the peace may issue out a warrant for searching in the day time any warehouse or house where the said goods are suspected to be lodged, and upon the pawnbroker refusing to open the same, any peace officer may break open the premises, doing no wilful damage, and the said goods shall be restored to the owner.

Pawnbrokers refusing to deliver up goods that have been pledged within the space of one year, the money lent with the interest thereon being tendered for the same, provided the principal does not exceed ten pounds, upon oath of such refusal, a justice is empowered to commit the pawnbroker to remain till the goods be delivered, or make satisfaction for the same.

Persons pawning goods not to be deemed owners, unless notice to the contrary, their having been pawned fraudulently or unjustly from the real owner.

Duplicates being lost, the owner thereof, upon oath before a justice declaring the goods to be his, a justice's certificate attending the loss, shall be entitled to another from the pawnbroker, for which, in case the money lent shall not exceed ten shillings, the pawnbroker shall receive one penny, if above ten shillings two pence, besides the same premium as when the goods were first pawned. Pawnbrokers receiving notice from the owners of goods, before the expiration of a year, shall not dispose of the said goods till th ter the expiration of three months to be computed from the expiration of the said year.

Goods to be sold by public auction after the expiration of one year, causing the same to be exposed to public view, and catalogues thereof to be published, and two advertisements giving notice of such sale, together with the name of the pawnbroker, to be inserted in some newspaper, two days at least before the first day of sale, upon pain of forfeiting for every offence five pounds to the owner of the said goods.

Pawnbrokers to enter an account of sales in their books, of all goods pawned for upwards of ten shillings, and in case of any overplus by the sale thereof, upon demand it shall be paid to the owner, provided such demand shall be made within three years after such sale, the necessary costs, principal and interest being deducted, and the persons who possess [illegible] entitled to the inspection of the book for the same one penny; and if [illegible] goods shall have sold for more than the sum entered, or such entry shall not have been made, or shall not [illegible] sold the same, or shall refuse to produce [illegible] shall for every such offence forfeit treble the sum the goods were originally pawned for, to be levied by distress.

Pawnbrokers shall not purchase goods while in their custody, or suffer them to be redeemed for that purpose, nor shall they take in pawn from any person who shall appear to be under twelve years of age, or to be intoxicated with liquor, or [illegible] any other [illegible] or buy any goods before the hour of eight in the forenoon, and after eleven in the evening; nor shall they receive any goods in pawn before eight o'clock in the forenoon, and after nine at night between Michaelmas and Lady Day, and before seven o'clock in the forenoon and after ten at night during the remainder of the year, excepting the evenings of Saturday, and the evenings preceding Good Friday and Christmas Day; nor shall any person carry on the trade of a pawnbroker on any Sunday, Good Friday, or Christmas Day.

Pawnbrokers are to place in view a table of rates

Pawnbroker's christian and surname and business to be written over the door, under a penalty of ten pounds, half to the informer.

Pawnbrokers having sold goods before the expiration of the time allowed by this act, or otherwise than according to the directions of this act, or have embezzled or have injured goods in any respect, justices shall award reasonable satisfaction to the owners of the said goods, in case the same shall not amount to the principal and profit thereon, but in case the satisfaction awarded shall be equal to or exceed the principal and profit, the goods shall be delivered to the owner without paying any principal and interest, under a penalty of ten pounds.

Pawnbrokers to produce their books before any justice if required, under a penalty of ten pounds.

Pawnbrokers neglecting to make their entry in a fair and regular manner shall upon complaint, forfeit ten pounds, and for every offence against this act where no penalty is provided the sum of five pounds, to be levied by distress and the informer shall be intitled to the sum of two pounds ten shillings, the remainder to the poor of the parish.

No person liable to a prosecution unless complaint shall be made within twelve months after the offence is committed.

Churchwardens to prosecute for every offence committed in that parish at the expence of the parish.

This act does not extend to persons lending money above ten pounds. Nor to extend to persons lending money upon goods at five per cent. interest.

Justices not to receive any fees or gratuities for acting under this act.

This act to extend to the executors, &c. of Pawnbrokers and Pawners.

A TABLE *of several* STAMPS, *with an account of the particulars for which they are used.*

The following are struck with Dies

Declaration, Plea, Replication, Rejoinder, Demurrer, or other pleadings whatsoever in any inferior Court of Law, and Copies thereof, 2d

Copies of Wills, Depositions in Chancery or other Courts of Equity at Westminster, Copy of any Bill, Answer, Plea, Demurrer, Replication, Rejoinder, Interrogatories, Depositions, or other Proceedings whatsoever in such Courts of Equity, Declaration, Plea, Replication, Rejoinder, Demurrer, or other Pleading whatsoever, in any Court of Law at Westminster, or in any of the Courts of the Principality of Wales, or in any of the Courts in the Counties Palatine of Chester, Lancaster, or Durham, and Copies thereof, 3d.

Parish Indentures, 6d.

Bill of Lading, [illegible]s.

Charity Children's Indentures, 1s.

Passports, Bail Bonds, and Assignments thereof, Surrender Certificates, 1s.

Ships first Registry, 1s.

Scotch Depositions, 1s.

Affidavit in any Court of Law or Equity at Westminster, or in any Court of the Great Sessions, for the Counties in Wales, or in the Court of the County Palatine of Chester, and Copies thereof, Common Bail to be filed in any Court of Law at Westminster, or in any of the aforesaid Courts, and upon the Appearance that shall be made upon such Bail, Rule or Order made or given in any of the Courts at Westminster, either Courts of Law or Equity, and Copies thereof, Entry of Actions for Forty Shillings and upwards, 1s. 6d.

Certificate or Debenture for Drawbacks, 2s.

Notarial Acts, Protest, Answer, Sentence and Final Decree, in Ecclesiastical Courts, the Courts of Admiralty, or Cinque Ports, and Copies thereof, and Copies of Citation or Monition, 2s.

Special Bail and Appearance thereon—Admission into Inns of Chancery, 2s.

Inventory or Catalogue of Furniture made with Reference to any Agreement, 2s. 6d.

Original Writ (unless Precipias) Subpoena, Bill of Middlesex, Latitat, Writ of Capias, Quo Minus, Writ of Dedimus Potestatem, every other Writ, Process or Mandate for Forty Shillings and upwards, 2s 6d

Citation or Monition, Libel or Allegation, Deposition or Inventory, exhibited in any Ecclesiastical Court, Courts of Admiralty, or Cinque Ports, and all Copies thereof, except Copies of Citation or Monition, which are not liable to the second additional Sixpence, 2s 6d

Bills, Answers, Replications, Rejoinders, Demurrers, Interrogatories, Depositions, taken by Commissions, and other Proceedings in Court of Equity, 2s 6d

Writ of Supersedeas, 3s

Matriculation in the Universities, 4s

Admission into Corporations or Companies, 4s.

Adjudication, Apprisings, Charter or Resignation, Confirmation, Novodamus or Charter upon Apprising or Adjudication, Principal or Original Retour of any Service of Heirs, or any Precept of Clare Constat, Seisin upon any Mortgage, Wadset, Heritable Bond, Alienation, Disposition, or upon any Charter, Instrument of Surrender, or Resignation of any Mortgages, &c. Service or Cognition of Heirs, Charter or Sesine of any Houses, Lands, &c. of Burgage Tenure in Scotland, 4s 6d

Scotch Letters and Bonds not given for the Security of Money, 5s

Awards, Certificate or Licence for Marriage, Writ of Habeas Corpus, Institution or Licence in Scotland, or any Writ or Instrument for the like purpose, 5s

Warrant, Monition, or personal Decree in Admiralty, or Cinque Port, Ecclesiastical Commission, Judgments, and Record of Nisi Prius and Postea, 5s

Agreements, 6s

N B *Twenty-one Days are allowed for Payment of the Duty on Agreements from the Date hereof*

Bond not given for the Security of Money, Charter party, Contract, Deed, or Deed Poll, Indenture, Obligatory Instrument, Letter of Attorney, Lease, Release, Articles of Clerkship, and Apprentices Indentures, 6s

CARDS AND DICE.

Cards per Pack 2s.

Dice per Pair, and all other Things used for any Game of Chance, 15s.

PAMPHLETS, NEWSPAPERS AND ALMANACKS.

Pamphlets of Half a Sheet or less, one halfpenny

Newspapers of Half a Sheet or less 1d

Pamphlets of One Sheet, 1d.

Newspapers of One Sheet, and for every additional Half Sheet of such Newspaper, 2d

Book Almanacks, 4d

Sheet Almanacks, 4d.

The Five following Duties are not expressed by any Stamp.

Pamphlets exceeding a Sheet, for every Sheet in One Copy of every Pamphlet, not exceeding Six Sheets in Octavo, or a lesser Size, Twelve Sheets in Quarto, and Twenty in Folio, 2s.

Every Advertisement in a Newspaper or periodical Pamphlet, 3s.

The Days and Hours of Transfer in the several Public Funds, with the Times when the Dividends become due.

	Days of Transfer	*Dividend when due*
Bank Stock - -	Tu. Thurf & Fri	La & Mi
5 per Cent Ann	Mon Wed. & Fri.	Mi. & Xs
4 per C. Con. 1780	Tu. Th. Fr & Sat.	La. & Mi
3 per Cent Conf	Tu. W Th & Fri	Mi & Xs
3 per Cent red	Tu W Th & Fri	La & Mi
3 per Cent 1726.	Tuefday & Thurf.	Mi & Xs
Long Annuities	Tu Wed & Sat.	Mi & Xs
Short ditto 1777	Wed. & Saturday	La & M
Conf. An. for 28 ys	Mon. Wed & Fri	Mi & Xs

South-Sea Stock	Mon. Wed. & Fri.	Mi. & Xs.
3 per C. Old Ann.	Mon. Wed. & Fri.	La. & Mi.
Ditto New Ann.	Tu. Thurs. & Sat.	Mi. & Xs.
Ditto 1751 - -	Tuesday & Thurs.	Mi. & Xs.
India Stock - -	Tu. Thurs. & Sat.	Mi. & Xs.
3 per Cent. Ann.	Mon. Wed. & Fri.	La. & Mi.

The Hours of Transferring at the Bank are from 11 o'Clock to 1. And the Hours for Payment of Dividends are from 9 to 11, and from 1 to 3 o'Clock.

The Hour of Transfer at the South Sea House is from 12 to 1 o'Clock. And the Hours for Dividends are from 9 till 12 o'Clock.

The Hour of Transfer at the East India House is from 12 to 1 o'Clock. And the Hours for Dividends are from 9 o'Clock till 2.

Holidays excepted.

HOLIDAYS now kept at the Bank.

*** *Six have been lately taken off.*

January 1, 6, 18, 25, 30.	July 25.
February 2, 24.	August 12, 24.
March 25.	September 2, 21, 22, 29.
April 23.	October 18, 26, 28.
May 1, 29.	November 1, 4, 5, 9, 30.
June 4, 11, 24, 29.	December 21, 25, 26, 27, 28.

Moveable Holidays.

Good Friday	Holy Thursday
East. Mo. Tu. and Wed.	Whit Mo. and Tu.

Dividends paid at the Bank from 9 to 11, and 1 to 3.

Transfers from 11 to 1.

Dividends at the S. S. and Ind. Houses from 9 to 12.

Transfers from 12 to 1.

Courts in Scotland, the great Sessions in Wales, or in any Courts in the Counties Palatine, or in any other Court holding Pleas to 40s or more 2s 6d

Every Solicitor, Attorney, Notary, Proctor, Agent, or Procurator, who shall reside in any of the Inns of Court or in the Cities of London and Westminster, the Borough of Southwark, the Parish of St Pancras, and St Mary-le-bone, or within the Bills of Mortality, or within the City of Edinburgh, 5l

Every Solicitor, Attorney, Notary, Proctor, Agent or Procurator, who shall reside in any other Part of Great Britain, 3l

BONDS

Bond given as Security for Money for 100l or under, 5s

If above the Sum of 100l and under 500l 10s

If of the Sum of 500l or upwards, 15s

BONDS given as Security for Money in SCOTLAND.

Bond given as a Security for Money, for 100l or under, 4s.

If above the Sum of 100l and under 500l 9s

If of the Sum of 500l or upwards, 1[illegible]

PROBATES OF WILLS AND LETTERS OF ADMINISTRATION

Of any Estate above 20l and under 100l 10s

If the Estate is of the Value of 100l and under 300l 2l 10s

If the Estate is of the Value of 300l and under 600l [illegible]l 10s

If the Estate is of the Value of 600l and under 1000l 8l

If the Estate is of the Value of 1000l and under 2000l 11l [illegible]

If the Estate is of the Value of 2000l and under 3000l 15l

If the Estate is of the Value of 300l and upwards, 20l (For Legacies see page 57)

APPRENTICE DUTY

Duty on Consideration Money given with Clerks and Apprentices, if 50l or under, Sixpence in the Pound, 6d

Duty on ditto, if above 50l One Shilling in the Pound, 1s

POLICIES

Policy of Assurance on House Goods, or Life Ship, Cargo or both with the Bills of Mortality, on any Sum not exceeding 1000l 5s

If above 1000l 1s

Policy of Assurance on House Goods or Life Ship, Cargo, or both, without the Bills of Mortality, on any Sum not exceeding 1000l 6s

If above 1000l 1s

Policy of Assurance on House Goods, or Life Ship, Cargo or both, on any Sum not exceeding 1000l in Scotland, 5s

If above 1000l in Scotland 10s

Note, On all Policies of Insurance from Loss by Fire, the Yearly Sum of 1s 6d *is payable on every* 100l *insured*

INSURANCE FROM FIRE

Insurance of Houses, Goods, &c from Fire, upon every 100l so insured, 1s 6d

REGISTRY OF BURIALS, &c

Entry of any Burial, Marriage, Birth, or Christening, in the Register of any Parish, Precinct, or Place in Great Britain, 3d.

CARDS AND DICE

Cards per Pack, 2s

Dice per Pair and all other Things used for any Game of Chance, 15s.

PAMPHLETS, NEWSPAPERS, AND ALMANACKS

Pamphlets of Half a Sheet or less, one halfpenny

News Papers of Half a Sheet or less, 1d

Pamphlets of One Sheet, 1d

News Papers of One Sheet, and for every additional half Sheet of such News Paper, [illegible]

Book Almanacks 4d

Sheet Almanacks, 1d

The Two following Duties are not expressed by any Stamp

Pamphlets exceeding a Sheet, for every Sheet in One Copy of every Pamphlet not exceeding Six Sheets in Octavo or a lesser Size, Twelve Sheets in Quarto, and Twenty in Folio, 2s

Every Advertisement in a Newspaper or periodical Pamphlet, 3s

---

The Days and Hours of Transfer at the several Public Funds with the Times when the Dividends become due

	Days of Transfer	Dividends due
Bank Stock - -	Tu. Thurs. & Fri.	La. & Mi.
5 per Cent. Ann.	Mon. W[illegible] & Fri.	Mi. & Xs
4 per Cent. Con. 1780	Tu. Th[illegible] & Sat.	La. & Mi.
3 per Cent. Con.	[illegible] W. Th. & Fri.	Mi. & Xs
[illegible] per Cent. red.	Tu. W. Th. & Fri.	La. & Mi.
3 per Cent. [illegible] 26	Tuesday & Thurs.	Mi. & Xs
Long A[illegible]	Tu. Wed. & Sat.	Mi. & Xs
Short [illegible]	Wed. & Saturday	La. & Mi.
Consol. An. for 2[illegible]	Mon. Wed. & Fri.	Mi. & Xs

South-Sea Stock	Mon. Wed. & Fri.	Mr & Xs
[illegible] Old [illegible]	Mon. Wed. & Fri.	[illegible] & Mr
Ditto New Ann.	Tu. Thurs. & Sat.	Mr & Xs
Ditto [illegible]	Tuesday & Thurs.	Mr & Xs
India Stock	Tu. Thurs. & Sat.	Mr & Xs
[illegible] Ann.	Mon. Wed. & Fri.	[illegible] & Mr

The Hours of Transferring at the Bank are from 11 [illegible] to 1. And the Hours for Payment of Dividends are from 9 to 11, and from 1 to 3 o'Clock.

The Hour of Transfer at the South Sea House [illegible] to 1 o'Clock. And the Hours for Dividends are from 9 till 12 o'clock.

The Hour of Transfer at the East India House is from 12 to 1 o'Clock. And the Hours for Dividends are from 9 o'Clock till 2.

Holidays excepted.

HOLIDAYS now kept at the Bank.

* *Such have been lately [illegible] off*

[illegible] 6, 18, [illegible]	July [illegible]
February 2, [illegible]	August [illegible]
March	September [illegible], 22, 29
April	October [illegible], 18, [illegible]
May [illegible]	November [illegible]
June [illegible] 29	December [illegible] 28

Moveable [illegible]

Good Friday	Holy Thursday
[illegible] Mon. Tu. and Wed.	Whit [illegible]

Dividends paid at the Bank from 9 to 11, and 1 t[illegible]

[illegible] is from 11 to 1

Dividends at the S. S. and Ind. Ho. from 9 to 12

[illegible] from 12 to 1

HOLIDAYS kept at the PUBLIC OFFICES

Months	HOLIDAYS	Exchequer	Stamp	Excise	Customs	S. S. House
January	Circumcision	K		K	K	K
	Epiphany	K	K	[illegible]	K	N
	Q. Charl. Birth day	K	[illegible]	K	K	K
	Conv. St Paul	K		[illegible]	[illegible]	K
	K. Charl. I. Mart.	K	[illegible]	K	K	K
Feb.	Purif. V. Mary	K	K	K	[illegible]	K
	Valentine	K	N	K		N
March	St David	K	N		N	N
	Shrove Tuesday	K	K	[illegible]	N	K
	Ash Wednesday	K			N	N
	Lady Day	K		[illegible]		K
April	Good Friday	K		[illegible]		K
	St George	K			N	N
	Easter Monday St M.	K	N	K		K
	Easter Tuesday	K	[illegible]	[illegible]		K
May	St Philip and James	K	K	[illegible]	[illegible]	K
	K. Charl. Birth-day	K	K	[illegible]		[illegible]
	Q. Elizabeth b.	N	N	N	N	N
	Charl. I. Rest	K	[illegible]	[illegible]		N
June	Holy Thursday	K	N	K		K
	K. Geo. III. born	K	[illegible]	K		K
	Pr. [illegible] Aug. b	K	[illegible]	K		K
	St Barnabas	K	N	K		N
	Whit Monday	K	K	K		K
	Whit Tuesday	K	K	[illegible]		K
	St John Bapt.	K	K	K	K	K
	St Peter and Paul	K	K	K	K	K
July	St James	K	N	K	N	N
August	Prs. [illegible] b	K	K	K	K	K
	Prs. of Brunswick b	K	K	K	K	K
	Pr. of Wales born	K	K	K	K	K
	Duke of York b	K	K	K	K	K
	Duke of Clarence b	K	K	K	K	K
	St. Bartholomew	K	K	K	N	N

Months	HOLIDAYS	Exchequer	Stamp	Excise	Customs	S. S. Trade
September	London burnt	K	K	K	K	[illegible]
	Holy Rood	[illegible]	N	K	N	[illegible]
	K. G. I & II land.	K	K	K	N	K
	St. Matthew	K	K	K	K	N
	K. G. III & Q. C. cor.	K	K	K	K	K
	St. Mic. & Prs. Ch. b.	K	K	K	K	[illegible]
October	St. Luke	[illegible]	[illegible]	K	K	K
	K. Geo. III Inaug.	K	K	K	N	K
	K. Geo. III Proc.	K	N	N	N	K
	St. Simon and Jude	K	K	K	[illegible]	[illegible]
November	All Saints	K	K	K	K	[illegible]
	All Souls	K	N	K	N	N
	K. William born	[illegible]	K	K	K	K
	Powder Plot	K	K	K	[illegible]	K
	Lord Mayor's Day[4]	N	K	K	K	[illegible]
	Q. Eliz. acced.	K	K	K	N	N
	D. of C[illegible] b.	N	K	N	N	[illegible]
	St. Andrew	K	K	K	[illegible]	[illegible]
December	St. Thomas	K	K	K	K	[illegible]
	Christmas Day	K	K	K	K	[illegible]
	St. Stephen	K	K	K	[illegible]	K
	St. John	K	K	K	[illegible]	[illegible]
	Holy Innocents	K	K	K	K	

*** K stands for kept, N for not kept, S for Saturday, S for Sunday

Useful Table, which exhibit the amount of [illegible] wages, [illegible] expences [illegible], salaries [illegible] annuities, for any [illegible] from one pound to one thousand pounds per annum.

By year	By month				By week				By day			
£	£	s	d	f	£	s	d	f	£	s	d	f
1	0	1	[illegible]	[illegible]	0	0	4	2	0	[illegible]	0	[illegible]
[illegible]	0	3	0	3	0	0	9	1	0	0	1	1
3	0	4	[illegible]	1	0	1	1	3	0	0	[illegible]	0
4	0	6	1		0	1	0	2	0	0	2	3
5	0	7	8	0	0	1	1	0	0	0	[illegible]	1
[illegible]	0	0	[illegible]	[illegible]	0	2	3	2	0	0	4	0
[illegible]	0	10	0	0	0	[illegible]	8	1	0	0	[illegible]	[illegible]
[illegible]	0	1[illegible]	[illegible]	1	0	3	0	0	0	0	[illegible]	1
[illegible]	0	13	9	0	0	3	0	[illegible]	0	0	6	0
10	0	1[illegible]	4	[illegible]	0	[illegible]	10	0	0	0	6	[illegible]
11	0	[illegible]	[illegible]	[illegible]	0	4	[illegible]		0	0	7	1
12	[illegible]	1[illegible]	0	0	0	4	[illegible]	1	0	0	8	0
13	0	10	11	1	0	4	11	3	0	0	8	2
14	1	1	[illegible]	3	0	0	4	2	0	0	[illegible]	1
15	1	3		1	0	[illegible]	9	0	0	0	[illegible]	
16	1	4	6	2	0	6	1	3	0	0	10	[illegible]
17	1	6	1	0	0	6	6	1	0	0	11	1
18	1	7	7	[illegible]	0	6	10	3	0	0	11	[illegible]
19	1	9	1	3	0	7	3	2	0	1	0	[illegible]
20	1	10	[illegible]	1	0	7	8	0	0	1	1	1
30	2	6	0	1	0	1[illegible]	6	0	0	1	7	3
40	3	1	4	2	0	15	4	0	0	2	2	1
50	3	16	8	2	0	19	2	1	0	2	0	0
60	4	12	0	[illegible]	1	[illegible]	0	1	0	3	3	[illegible]
70		[illegible]	4	[illegible]	1	6	10	1	0	[illegible]	1[illegible]	0
80	6	[illegible]	0	0	1	10	8	1	0	[illegible]	[illegible]	2
90	6	18	1	0	1	14	6	1	0	[illegible]	1[illegible]	1
100	7	13	[illegible]	0	1	18	[illegible]	1	0	[illegible]	[illegible]	[illegible]
200	15	6	10	1	3	16	8	2	0	10	11	2
300	23	0	3	1	5	15	0	3	0	16	[illegible]	1
400	30	13	8	[illegible]	7	13	0	0	1	1	11	0
500	38	7	1	2	9	11	9	1	1	[illegible]	1	3
1000	76	14	3	0	19	3	0	3	2	14	9	2

By the days			By the week				By the month			By the year			
s	d	f	£	s	d	f	£	s	d	£	s	d	f
0	0	1	0	0	1	3	0	0	7	0	7	7	1
0	0	2	0	0	3	2	0	1	2	0	15	2	2
0	0	3	0	0	5	1	0	1	9	1	2	9	3
0	1		0	0	7		0	2	4	1	10	5	
0	2		0	1	2		0	4	8	3	0	10	
0	3		0	1	9		0	7	0	4	11	3	
0	4		0	2	4		0	9	4	6	1	8	
0	5		0	2	11		0	11	8	7	12	[illegible]	
0	6		0	3	6		0	1	0	9	2	6	
0	7		0	4	1		0	16	4	10	12	11	
0	8		0	4	8		0	18	8	12	3	4	
0	9		0	5	3		1	1	0	13	13	9	
0	10		0	5	10		1	3	4	15	4	2	
0	11		0	6	5		1	5	8	16	14	7	
1	0		0	7	0		1	8	0	18	5	0	
2	0		0	14	0		2	16	0	36	10	0	
3	0		1	1	0		4	4	0	54	15	0	
4	0		1	8	0		5	12	0	73	0	0	
5	0		1	15	0		7	0	0	91	5	0	
6	0		2	2	0		8	8	0	109	10	0	
7	0		2	9	0		9	16	0	127	15	0	
8	0		2	16	0		11	4	0	146	0	0	
9	0		3	3	0		12	12	0	164	5	0	
10	0		3	10	0		14	0	0	182	10	0	
11	0		3	17	0		15	8	0	200	15	0	
12	0		4	4	0		16	16	0	219	0	0	
13	0		4	11	0		18	4	0	237	5	0	
14	0		4	18	0		19	12	0	255	10	0	
15	0		5	5	0		21	0	0	273	15	0	
16	0		5	12	0		22	8	0	292	0	0	
17	0		5	19	0		23	16	0	310	5	0	
18	0		6	6	0		25	4	0	328	10	0	
19	0		6	13	0		26	12	0	346	15	0	
20	0		7	0	0		28	0	0	365	0	0	

N B In these tables, the month is only 28 days

ACTS NOT RELATING TO THE TAXES

Carts and Drays, in and within five miles of London

NO perſon ſhall drive any cart, dray, &c within five miles of Temple Bar, or in the bills of mortality, except the owner ſhall have entered his name and abode at the hackney coach office, and affix his name and number on ſome conſpicuous part thereof or be ſubject to all the penalties created by any laws now in being relative to ſuch owners of carts, &c

---

CHIMNEY SWEEPERS, *and their Apprentices*

(28 *Geo* III)

FROM and after the 5th of July, 1788, all church wardens and overſeers in every part of Great Britain for the time being, may, with the conſent or approbation of two or more juſtices (ſuch conſent being ſigned by ſuch juſtices in their hand writing), bind or put out any boys eight years old or upwards, who are chargeable to the pariſh, or whoſe parents ſhall become chargeable to the pariſh where they ſhall ſo be, or who ſhall beg for alms, or by or with the conſent of the parent or parents of ſuch boy or boys, to be apprenticed to any perſon uſing the trade of a ſweep chimney for ſo long a time, and until ſuch boy ſhall attain the age of 16 years, which binding ſhall be as effectual in the law as if he were of full age, and by indenture had bound himſelf

Their age at the time of binding to be mentioned in the indenture, which muſt be extracted from the regiſter of their baptiſm, and atteſted by the miniſter without fee or reward, upon paper or parchment unſtamped

Where no ſuch copy or regiſter of baptiſm can be had, the juſtices are to inform themſelves as well as they can, of their age, and inſert it in their indenture

Maſters taking apprentices under eight years of age or neglecting the above form, forfeit not leſs than 5l or more than 10l.

Justices are to hear and determine all complaints against either masters or boys.

No person to have more than six apprentices at once, each of them to wear a brass plate in the front of a leathern cap with the name and place of abode of the master or mistress, neglect in this case, or having more than six apprentices at once is the same penalty, the like penalty also for using boys ill or breaking any of the covenants of the indenture.

Boys are not to be let out for hire, neither are they to call the streets before seven in the morning, nor after twelve at noon, between Michaelmas and Lady-Day, nor before five in the morning, nor after twelve at noon between Lady Day and Michaelmas, under the like forfeiture. Conviction of penalties to be made by one or more credible persons, before one or more justices acting for the place where the offence is committed.

Penalties to be levied if not regularly paid upon conviction, with all costs and charges by distress and sale of goods one half to the informer and the other half to the poor.

If there are no effects to pay the penalties and costs, the party must be sent to prison for any time not exceeding three months, unless the penalty should be paid sooner.

Appeals for supposed grievances must be made at the next quarter sessions belonging to the place where the complaint shall arise.

COURTS OF CONSCIENCE

Act relative to Prisoners committed by the Courts of Conscience in London, Middlesex and the Borough of Southwark, to prevent long confinement and the payment of fees. (25 Geo III c 45)

FROM the 24th of June, 1785, no person committed for debt by any order or process of the Courts of Conscience in the above places, viz. the city of London, the Borough of Southwark, and the county of

Middlesex, which includes Westminster, shall continue in confinement longer than 20 days where the debt is not above 20s. and where the debt is above 20s and does not exceed 40s they shall not be confined more than 40 days

When the time of confinement expires they are to be discharged without paying any fee reward, or gratuity whatsoever, and every goaler or turnkey confining them longer upon any pretence or demanding any fee reward, or gratuity whatsoever, shall forfeit 5l

Complaints of offences to be made within two months one half of the penalty to the poor of the parish, the other to the informer Two justices may determine the matter

No persons in future to act as Commissioners of the different Courts of Conscience unless they are housholders within the district city, liberty, or place they are to act in and they shall also be possessed of a real estate of 20l per annum, or a personal estate of the value of 500l

Persons presuming to act who are not so qualified, forfeit 20l. provided the action is brought within six months.

By an act of the 26th of Geo. III c 38 all the Courts of Conscience in the kingdom are put exactly under the same regulations

---

HACKNEY-COACHES

Abstract of the several Acts of Parliament relating to Hackney Coaches

THE King may appoint a number of Commissioners, not exceeding five, to licence and regulate Hackney-Coaches within the cities of London and Westminster the suburbs [illegible] and other places within the bills of [illegible] not exceeding 1000 every proprietor paying * ten shillings per week by monthly payments

* *This is [illegible] additional duty of five shillings [illegible] from the 1st of Sept 1784*

Every coach ſhall have its number on each ſide, and if any proprietor ſhall preſume to alter his number, he ſhall forfeit 5l. half to the king, and half to the informer.

The horſes to be uſed with Hackney Coaches ſhall not be under 14 hands high.

No perſon ſhall drive or let to hire any Hackney-Coach without licence, on pain of 5l. and from and after the 4th of September 1784, if any perſon ſhall drive a mourning coach or hearſe to any funeral within the cities of London and Weſtminſter, or the ſuburbs thereof, or within five miles of Temple Bar, without a licenced number fixed on its fore ſtandard, he ſhall be liable to a penalty of 5l.

Any coachman plying for hire, may be obliged, on every day of the week, to go at reaſonable times any where within the diſtance of ten miles from the city of London or Weſtminſter; and if he has not a checque-ſtring placed in a proper part of his coach, ſhall forfeit five ſhillings.

If the owners of Hackney Coaches, or their proper drivers, neglect to attend the Commiſſioners upon third ſummons, they ſhall forfeit their licence.

From and after the 1ſt of Auguſt 1786, the ſeveral Rates or Fares formerly paid, were repealed, and the following ſubſtituted in their ſtead.

For any diſtance not exceeding 1 mile and one quarter, 1s.

Above 1 mile and one quarter, and not exceeding 2 miles, 1s. 6d.

Above 2 miles, and not exceeding 2 miles and one half, 2s.

Above 2 miles and one half, and not exceeding 3 miles, 2s. 6d.

Above 3 miles, and not exceeding 3 miles and one half, 3s.

Above 3 miles and one half, and not exceeding 4 miles, 3s. 6d.

Above 4 miles, and not exceeding 4 miles and one half, 4s.

Above 4 miles and one half, and not exceeding 5 miles, 4s. 6d.

And so on to the extent of 10 miles from London or Westminster, at the rate of sixpence for each additional half mile, the last of which is to be paid if entered upon.

If the coach is kept in waiting, or paid by time, the fares will be

			s	d
For any time not exceeding 3 quar. of an hour,			1	0
From 3 quar. of an hour, and not exceeding 1 hour,			1	6
From 1 hour 00 min.	—	to 1 hour 20 min.	2	0
From 1 hour 20 min.	—	to 1 hour 40 min.	2	6
From 1 hour 40 min.	—	to 2 hours 00 min.	3	0
From 2 hours 00 min.	—	to 2 hours 20 min.	3	6
From 2 hours 20 min.	—	to 2 hours 40 min.	4	0
From 2 hours 40 min.	—	to 3 hours 00 min.	[illegible]	6
From 3 hours 00 min.	—	to 3 hours 20 min.	5	0
From 3 hours 20 min.	—	to 3 hours 40 min.	5	6
From 3 hours 40 min.	—	to 4 hours 00 min.	6	0
From 4 hours 00 min.	—	to 4 hours 20 min.	6	6
From 4 hours 20 min.	—	to 4 hours 40 min.	7	0
From 4 hours 40 min.	—	to 5 hours 00 min.	7	6

And so on for any additional time at the rate of sixpence for every 20 minutes, the last of which is to be paid for if entered upon.

For a day of 12 hours - - - - - £ 0 14 6

For any time after the said 12 hours the coach is to be considered as a coach in waiting, and paid for accordingly.

All the space betwixt the Stand and the taking up of the fare is to be reckoned into the fare, and the coachman at liberty to take either for the length of ground or time, but not for both, nor can he charge more than one shilling for any time within the first quarters of an hour, unless he has gone above one mile and a quarter, his stopping and waiting at various places, driving slow by desire, or returning from whence he came, make no addition to the fare.

Any coachman refusing to go at, or exacting more for his hire than according to the foregoing rates, shall forfeit a sum not exceeding 3l. or under 10s. and in case of misbehaviour by abusive language or other wise the Commissioners may revoke his licence, or inflict a penalty not exceeding 3l to the poor, and on non-payment, to be committed and kept to hard labour for 30 days

Any person refusing to pay the fare, or defacing the coach, may be brought by warrant before any justice, who, on proof upon oath, may award satisfaction to the party, and in case of refusal to pay, may bind him over to the next sessions

Rents and penalties to be levied by distress, and in default thereof, imprisonment till paid, and if any rent is fourteen days unpaid, the licence may be withdrawn

The following are the common Stands at present in use but a coach may stand and ply in any street that is 30 feet in width from curve to curve, (except St. James's street and Pall mall) the following regulations observed

That not more than 8 Hackney Coaches shall stand at a time (in Cornhill) of those seven between the end of Gracechurch street and Finch lane, and one between Freeman's court and Finch lane

In Leadenhall street, three coaches and no more may stand between the west end of the India house, and the passage leading to the Green market

In Cheapside, between Bucklersbury and Iron monger lane, three coaches

In King street Cheapside, five coaches three from the end of Trump street towards Cateaton street, and two from Trump street towards Cheapside

In Aldermanbury only four, viz two in the broad part, near the church, and two at the East end of the church

At the west end of St Paul's only one

In Fleet street, between Temple bar and Chancery lane, only two coaches and not more than one between the said lane and the west end of St. Dunstan's church

A coach should be taken possession of, before the coachman is told where to drive if he then refuses to proceed he is liable to be punished, and if at any time you apprehend that more than the proper fare is demanded, you may offer whatever is asked, but charge the coachman to take no more than is due, and if he then persists in the overcharge and takes it, you may take his number and apply for redress at the Hackney-Coach office in Somerset Place

†‡† The Alderman of every ward of the city and every justice of the peace in the said cities and counties may inflict and levy the like penalties for any offences contrary to this act, as the Commissioners may Provided that no person be punished twice for the same offence

, All Hackney-coachmen are to take care not to place their coaches nearer to each other than twelve yards nor within twelve yards of any cross street.— Any coachman presuming to place his coach otherwise than is hereby directed or exceeding the number in those places which are limited, will be fined for every offence ten shillings

An Admeasurement of the most common One Shilling and Eighteen Penny Fares to be taken by Hackney coachmen for their hire in and about the cities of London and Westminster and places adjoining, under the new act of the 26th of Geo III 72

ONE SHILLING FARES

The distance not exceeding one mile and two furlongs, or one mile and a quarter

From what Stand

Palace Yard Westminster —Westminster Hall Gate to the first coach at St Clement's Strand, to the end of St James's street, Piccadilly

Whitehall —The centre of the Horse Guards, to Water Lane, Fleet street

To the end of Engine-street, Piccadilly

Charing Cross —The Golden Cross, to Hamilton street Piccadilly

To the Old Bailey or Ludgate-hill

Strand —Catharine street, Strand, to Bow Church-yard, Cheapside

From what
Stand

Temple Bar—The west side, to Derby-street, Parliament street
To Birch lane Cornhill

Bridge street, Fleet street—The first coach, to Creechurch lane, Leadenhall street
To opposite Craig's-court Charing Cross

St Paul's—The first coach, to Hungerford market, Strand
To opposite the Blue Post Whitechapel

Cheapside.—Gutter lane, to Southampton street Holborn
To Church lane, Whitechapel-road

Cornhill—The centre of the Royal Exchange, to Grey Hound lane, Whitechapel
To opposite Palfgrave head-court Strand
To opposite Gray's Inn Gate, Holborn

Whitechapel—The first coach near the Three Nuns, To the first White Horse-lane, Mile End Road
To the end of Avemary lane, Ludgate hill

Holborn—The end of Hatton-garden, to Lime-street, Leadenhall-street
To the end of Dean street Oxford street
To the end of Southampton Buildings, Johnson's Court, Charing Cross
To the centre of the Royal Exchange
The end of Red Lion street to the centre of The Horse Guards, Whitehall
The Vine Tavern, to Bow Church-yard, Cheapside
To the end of Shepherd-street Oxford street

Oxford street The end of Rathbone-place, to the end of Paddington-road
To the end of Shoe-lane, Holborn
The end of Bond street, to the end of Little Queen street Holborn
The end of Park-street, to the end of Denmark-street St. Giles's

Piccadilly—The Golden Lion, to Chandos-street, St. Martin's Lane

From what
Stand

To th Mews Gate, Charing Cross
To the end of St. James's Street, to Somer's Coffee house, Strand
To the Ordnance Office, St Margaret's street, Westminster
The coach next the Haymarket, to Vine street, Milbank-street
Tower-hill—The first coach, to the Bell Savage, Ludgate-hill
King-street, Cheapside—Catenton street, to Surry-street Strand
To opposite Featherstone Buildings, Holborn
Clerkenwell Green—Opposite the Close, to the Mansion House
Buckingham Gate—Opposite the gate to the gate of Northumberland House Strand
To the end of Turk's row, in Burton's row, Chelsea.

EIGHTEEN PENNY FARES

The distance not exceeding Two miles

From what
Stand

Palace Yard, Westminster—Westminster Hall Gate, To Watling street St Paul's Church yard,
To opposite the Horse Guards, at Knightsbridge
Whitehall.—The centre of the Horse Guards, to Mercers Chapel in Cheapside
To the end of Bear court Knightsbridge
Charing Cross.—The Golden Cross, to Smith's Manufactory, Knightsbridge
To Bank street Cornhill
Strand.—Catherine-street, Strand, to Poor Jury street, Aldgate
Temple Bar—The west side, to Grosvenor House, Milbank-row, Westminster
Temple Bar—To the Red Lion and Spread Eagle Whitechapel

From what
Stand,

Bridge street, Fleet street—The first coach, to the New Road, Whitechapel Road

To the turning to Queen-square Westminster

St Paul's—The first coach, to St James's Palace Gate

To the sign of the London Hospital

Cheapside—Gutter-lane, to the end of Poland street, Oxford-road

To the end of Button-lane, Mile End Road

Cornhill—The corner of the Royal Exchange, to the Rose and Crown, Mile End Road

To the end of St Martin's-lane

To the end of Denmark street, St Giles's

Whitechapel—The first coach near the Three Nuns, To the Road leading to Bow Common,

To Somerset House

Holborn—The end of Hatton Garden, to the end of Garden street, Whitechapel-road

To the end of Duke street, Oxford street

The end of Southampton-buildings, to the end of Dartmouth street, Tothil street, Westminster

To the Red Lion and Spread Eagle, Whitechapel

The end of Red Lion-street to the King's Head Lambeth marsh

The Vine Tavern to the end of Poor-Jury street Aldgate

To Tyburn Turnpike

Oxford street—The end of Rathbone Place to the end of Bigg's lane, in the road to Bayswater

To the end of the Old Jury, Poultry

The end of Bond street, to the end of Cow lane, Snow-hill

The end of Park street, to Gray's Inn Gate, Holborn

Piccadilly—The Golden Lion, to Palsgrave-head court, Temple Bar

To the end of Wood street, Milbank street, Westminster

From what Stand

The end of St. James's-street, to the first coach in St Paul's church-yard

Tower-hill—The first coach, to the centre of Exeter 'Change, Strand

King-street, Cheapside—Catcaton-street, to the end of Suffolk street, Cockspur street

To the Boar and Castle, Oxford-street.

Clerkenwell Close—Opposite the Close, to the Talbot Inn, Whitechapel

Buckingham Gate—Opposite the Gate, to the end of Essex street, Strand

To the [illegible], China-row, Chelsea.

By order of the Commissioners,

EDWARD MOORE, Register

Hackney-Coach Office, Somerset House,
July 21, 1786

N. B. These distances are measured from one specific point of ground to another, as above, but upon a question, there will be added the call of the coach, together with any other necessary departure from the right line.

EDINBURGH FARES OF HACKNEY-COACHES,

Excluding Tolls and King's Duty

	£	s	d
FROM any part of the city to another, or any part of the New Town, or suburbs,	0	1	0
One hours attendance and to return	0	1	6
From Hanover-street, and other parts of the New Town westward of that street, to the Cannongate below, or to the eastward of St John's-cross, or to Nicholson's-street, or other parts of the suburbs on the south,	0	1	6
One hour's attendance, and to return,	0	2	0
For every hour's attendance after the first,	0	1	0

On time, within the city and suburbs

For the first hour, 0 1 6
For every after hour, 0 1 0
In case a coach be detained before using it, for every half-hour, in addition to the fare 0 0 6
From the south end of North Bridge street, or from any part of the New Town, east of Hanover street to Leith, 0 1 6
One hour's attendance, and to return 0 2 6
From any part of the High street or south of it, or from Hanover-street or west of it to Leith, 0 2 0
One hour's attendance, and to return 0 3 0
From the south end of North Bridge street, and from the eastward of Hanover street to Broughton, Antigua-street, or the like distance, 0 1 0
One hour's attendance and to return, 0 1 6
From any other part of the city or suburbs 0 1 6
One hour's attendance, and to return, 0 2 0
From the south end of North Bridge-street, or any part of the New Town, to Drumsheugh, including the whole houses to Brichead, or any part of the like distance, 0 1 0
One hour's attendance, and to return, 0 1 6
From any other part of the city or suburbs, 0 1 6
One hour's attendance and to return, 0 2 0
To any place within the Whitehouse toll, farther than Drumsheugh, 6d. in addition to each of the four last mentioned fares
From any part of the Old Town to Gibbet or Grange-toll, or the like distance 0 1 6
One hour's attendance, and to return, 0 2 0
From any part of the New Town to Gibbet or Grange toll, or the like distance 0 2 0
One hour's attendance and to return, 0 2 6
To any of the following places setting down viz. Dean, Dalry, Merchiston, east and west Grange, Powburn, Restalrig, Murrayfield, &c. 0 2 0
Two hour's attendance, and to return, 0 [illegible] 0
Every hours attendance, after the first two, 0 1 0

To any of the following places, ſetting down, viz. Newhaven, Bellmount, Gorgie, Blackford, &c	0	2	6
Two hour's attendance, and to return,	0	4	0
To every hour's attendance after the firſt two,	0	1	0
To the following places, ſetting down, viz Dryslaw, Coſtorphine, Saughton hall, Slateford, &c	0	3	6
Two hour's attendance, and to return,	0	5	0
Every hour's attendance after the firſt two,	0	1	0
To any of the following places, ſetting down, viz. Niddry, Edmonſtone Somervell-houſe, &c	0	5	0
Two hour's attendance, and to return,	0	7	0
Every hour after the firſt two,	0	1	0
To any of the following places, ſetting down, viz. Cramond, Currie, Mavisbank, Laſswade, &c.	0	7	0
Three hour's attendance, and to return,	0	9	0
Every hour attendance after the firſt three,	0	1	0
To any of the following places, ſetting down, viz Smeaton, Polton, Newbottle, Roſlin, &c	0	8	0
Three hour's attendance and to return,	0	10	0
Every hour after the firſt three	0	1	0
To any of the following places, ſetting down, viz. Preſtonpans, Kirkliſton, Newliſton, &c	0	10	0
Three hour's attendance, and to return,	0	12	0
Every hour's attendance after the firſt three	0	1	0
To any of the following places, ſetting down, viz Arniſton, Tranent, Elphinſton, Queensferry, &c.	0	12	0
Three hour's attendance, and to return,	0	16	0
Every hour's attendance after the firſt three,	0	1	0
To any of the following places, ſetting down, viz. Ormiſton, Crichton, Borthwick,	0	14	0
Three hour's attendance and to return,	0	16	0
To do. every hour's attendance after the firſt three,	0	1	0
To ditto for above eight, and not exceeding ten miles, going and returning ſame day	1	0	

HACKNEY CHAIRS

	£	s	d
EVERY lift within the ancient royalty including the Canongate as far as the British Linen Office, and the street of Potterrow,	0	0	6
Ditto to St Andrew's Square, Theatre and adjacent buildings in the extended royalty,	0	0	6
Each lift from Edinburgh to Leith in the day-time,	0	2	6
Ditto in the night-time,	0	3	0
Hire for a forenoon,	0	2	6
Hire for an afternoon,	0	3	0
But if carried home after supper,	0	3	6
Hire for a whole day	0	4	6
Hire for a week,	1	5	0
Each hour's attendance,	0	0	6
Every lift after One o'clock in the morning,	0	1	0

Every double lift to pay double hire — Two Children, or One Child in a person's arms always excepted.

*** The last Regulation for Chairs, which took place the 23d of February 1791, is so extensively enumerated, as to prevent our inserting the whole in this work. Masters or Owners of Chairs, or their servants, are thereby obliged to produce a Printed Copy of said Regulations to their Employer if demanded, on pain of forfeiting their hire, and a penalty of Two Shillings and Sixpence for every offence

MAILS

THE Mail for London and all over England, departs with the Royal Mail Coach every afternoon at half past three o'clock Thursday excepted, and reaches London early in the morning of the third day after — Arrives every morning Wednesday excepted Postage to London, 7d

A mail is dispatched every Thursday for the places north of London, and a mail arrives from these places every Wednesday

The mails for North America, and the West Indies are made up on Saturday before the first Wednesday of every month Postage 1s 7d —and may or may not be paid to the West Indies, but to North America, must be paid at ingiving

Tuesdays and Saturdays are the proper days for giving in Letters to the Continent of Europe, and the arrivals are Mondays and Thursdays

There must be paid at Edinburgh, with all Foreign Letters as follows

To Holland, France, Flanders, and East-Indies, 1d

To Spain, Portugal, and Gibralter, 2s 1d.—Port-Mahon 1s 10d

To Italy, Sicily Turkey, Germany Geneva, Switzerland, Denmark, Sweden, and Russia, 1s 7d

N B An other attends day and night at the General Post Office, to dispatch expresses to any part of Britain

To *Leith*—Three Coaches go from the Cross of Edinburgh to the shore of Leith every half hour Tickets 1d halfpenny

From *Dalkeith*—Two Coaches every morning (Sundays excepted) at nine o'clock and return from the cross at eleven, come back at four afternoon in winter and five in summer, and leave Edinburgh in winter at six, and in summer at seven, in the evening, Tickets 1s 3d

From *Musselburgh*—Four coaches every morning at nine o'clock and five in the afternoon in summer, and four in winter, and return, two at eleven, one at twelve and another at one and six in winter, and seven in summer Tickets 1s.

From *Prestonpans*—One every morning at nine o'clock, and returns at three in winter, and four in summer, from Stewart's, High Street Tickets 1s 6d.

To and from *Haddington*—One every day at ten o'clock, from Duguid's at the cross Tickets 3s

To *Dunbar*—One from Walker's, head of Bell's wynd every Monday and Friday, at ten in the morning and returns every Tuesday and Saturday same hour Tickets 6s

To *Peebles*—One from Archibald's, Candlemaker row every Monday Wednesday, and Friday in summer, and Tuesday and Friday in winter, at nine in the morning, return same days. Tickets 5s.

To and from *Glasgow*.—One every morning at eight o'clock from Robertson's, Leith Walk, and Dick's, Glasgow Fare 8s Another at the same hour from Marshall's, Cowgate head, and Campell s, Grassmarket, and Paton s Glasgow Fare 8s Another at the same hour from Montgomery's, Grassmarket, and Dunbar's, Glasgow Fare 8s.—Another at the same hour from Cameron's Grassmarket, and Durie's, Glasgow Fare 8s Another every morning at nine o'clock from Warden's, Grassmarket, and Buchanan s, Glasgow Fare 10s 6d — Another every morning at eleven o'clock from Cameron's, Grassmarket, and Durie's, Glasgow Fare 10s 6d

To *Stirling*—One from Cameron's, Grassmarket, every Tuesday Thursday, and Saturday, returns from M'Kechnie's, Stirling, every Monday, Wednesday, and Friday, at eight in the morning Tickets 6s. Another from Mrs Gibson's, Grassmarket, every Monday, Wednesday, and Friday returns every Tuesday, Thursday, and Saturday, from Wingate's, same hour Tickets 9s 6d.

To *Berwick*—A Diligence sets out from D M'Farlane's every day, and from G Hall's, Berwick, at seven o'clock in the morning Tickets 1*l* 8d

To *London by Berwick*—The Royal Mail Coach sets out from Drysdale's, St Andrew's street, New Town, every afternoon at half past three o clock, arrives at Newcastle next morning at eight, and joins the Royal Mail Coach for London by way of Leeds To Newcastle, 1*l* 8s To York 2*l* 4s. To London, 4*l* 10s

The Royal Charlotte Post Coach sets out from Robertson's, head of Leith Walk, every morning at three o clock. Tickets to London 5*l* 7s.

To *Dumfries, Carlisle, and Portpatrick*—The Royal Mail Coach sets out from Drysdale's, Turf Coffe-house, every day at ten o'clock in the morning

To and from *Queensferry*—One every morning at nine, and four in the afternoon, from Warden's, Grassmarket Tickets 2s

To *Perth*—One every Tuesday, Thursday and Saturday from Robertson's Leith Walk at nine in the morning, returns every Monday, Wednesday, and Friday, at seven o'clock. Tickets 11s. 6d.

To *Aberdeen*, by Perth and Brechin.—One goes from Robertson's, Leith Walk, every Tuesday, Thursday, and Saturday, at ten in the forenoon, and from Aberdeen every Monday, Wednesday, and Friday, at four in the morning. Tickets 2l. 2s.

Jedburgh by Lauder.—One from Atkinson's Bristo Port, every Wednesday and Saturday, at six o'clock in the morning. Fare 11s. 6d.

To *Kelso*.—One from Dunibreck's, Canongate head every Tuesday, Thursday, and Saturday, at eight in the morning. Fare 13s.

To *Linlithgow* and *Falkirk*.—One every day from Marshall's, Cowgatehead, at four o'clock in the afternoon. Returns from Falkirk every morning at six o'clock. Tickets to Lithgow 3s. 6d. To Falkirk 5s.

*** The above departures, &c. are frequently altered.

LIST OF HIS MAJESTY's MAIL COACHES,

Which set out on the week days at eight, and on Sunday at seven in the evening, with the inns they go from.

BANBURY, *Oxfordshire*. From the George and Blue Boar, Holborn.

Bath and *Bristol*. From the Swan, Lad Lane, through Hounslow, Maidenhead, Reading, Newbury, Hungerford, Marlbro', Devizes, Calne, and Chippenham, and continued to Wells, Glastonbury, Bridgewater, Taunton, Wellington, and Exeter.

Carmarthen, Milford Haven, and *Huberstone*. From Swan, Lad Lane.

Chester and *Holyhead*. From the Golden Cross, Charing Cross, through Stafford, Ware, Namptwich, Tarporley, Holywell, Conway, and Bangor.

Carlisle. From Swan, Lad Lane, through Penrith, Kendal, and Lancaster.

Dover. From the George and Blue Boar, Holborn, through Dartford, Rochester, Chatham, Canterbury

Margate, Ramsgate, Deal, Sandwich, Folkstone, Feversham, and Sittenbourn

Edinburgh From the Bull and Mouth, near Aldersgate Street, through Ware, Buntingford, Royston, Caxton, Huntingdon, Aukingbury Hill, Stilton, Windesford, Stamford, Witham Common, Colsterworth, Grantham, Newark, Tuxford Retford Barnaby Moor, Bawtry, Doncaster, Ferrybridge, Milford, Tadcaster, (York,) Northallerton, Darlington, Durham Newcastle, and Berwick on Tweed

Exeter From the Swan Lad Lane, through Basingstoke, Andover, Salisbury, Blandford, Dorchester Bridport, Axminster, and Honiton

Hull From Bull and Mouth, near Aldersgate Street, through York and Beverley

Liverpool From the Swan, Lad Lane, through Prescot, Warrington, Knutsford, Congleton, Newcastle under Line, Stone, Litchfield, Wolseley Bridge, Ridgeley Meriden, Coventry, Dunchurch, Daventry, Towcester, Foster's Booth, Stoney Stratford, Fenny Stratford, and Brickhill

Manchester and *Derby* From the Swan, Lad Lane, through New Haven, Buxton, Stockport, Ashbourn, Loughborough, Leicester, Harborough, Northampton, and Newport Pagnell

Macclesfield and *Leek* From ditto

Margate and *Ramsgate* From George and Blue Boar, High Holborn, through Dartford, Chatham, Rochester Sittingbourn, and Canterbury

Norwich From the White Horse, Fetter Lane, through Illford, Romford, Brentwood, Ingatestone, Chelmsford, Witham, Kelvedon, Colchester Ipswich, Stoneham Scole Inn, and Long Stratton

Norwich and *Yarmouth* From the White Horse, Fetter Lane, through Epping, Harlow, Hockerhill, Littleburgh, Bournbridge, Newmarket, Barton mills Thetford, Larlingford, Attleborough, and Wymondham

Nottingham and *Leeds* From George and Blue Boar, Holborn, through St Alban's, Newport, Dunstable, Wooburn, Northampton, Harborough, Leicester,

Loughborough, Mansfield, Chesterfield, Sheffield, Barnsley, and Wakefield.

Oxford From Bull and Mouth, near Aldersgate Street, through Hounslow, Colnbrook, Slough, Maidenhead and Henley

Plymouth and *Falmouth* From the Swan, Lad Lane, through Basingstoke, Andover, Salisbury, Blandford, Dorchester, Bridport, Axminster, Honiton, and Exeter

Portsmouth From the Angel behind St Clement's, through Kingston, Esher, Cobham Ripley, Guildford, Godalming, Liphook, and Petersfield

Shrewsbury Brimingham, Kiddermunster, and *Bewdley* From the Bull and Mouth near Aldersgate Street through Southall, Uxbridge, Beaconsfield, High Wycomb, Tetsworth, Wheatley, Oxford, Woodstock, Shipston upon Stour, Henley in Arden, Wolverhampton, Shiffnall Stratford upon Avon, Chapel House, Bilstone, and Wellington

Southampton and *Poole* From Bell and Crown, Holborn, through Staines, Bagshot, Alton, Alresford, Winchester, Lindhurst, Lymington, Ringwood, and Wimbourn

Swansea and *Neath* From the Swan, Lad Lane, through Newbury, Wellington, Marlborough, Devizes Calne, Chippenham, Bath, Bristol, Newport, Cardiff, Cowbridge, and Pyle

Worcester and *Ludlow* From the George and Blue Boar, in Holborn, through Hounslow Colnbrook, Maidenhead, Henley, Nettlebed, Oxford, Woodstock, Enston, Chipping-Norton, Morton in the Marsh, Evesham, Pershore, Tenbury Broadway, and Bungworth.

York, Newcastle and *Edinburgh* From the Bull and Mouth near Aldersgate Street, through Stamford, Grantham, Newark, Doncaster, and Ferrybridge.

USEFUL REGULATIONS

For Edinburgh and Leith

CUSTOM OF A MERK

On the Pack of all English and Foreign Goods, (English wool excepted) brought into the city of Edinburgh and liberties thereof

	Scots.
FOR each horse pack consisting of eighteen stone Troy weight, and proportionably for packs or quantities of lesser weight £.	0 13 4
Each cart draught, drawn by one or more horses, for each horse drawing therein,	0 13 4
Each hogshead of liquor, tobacco, or other goods,	0 13 4
Each horse load of liquor in bottles or other casks	0 6 8

Goods carried off the road in order to evade custom, upon conviction thereof, are liable in payment of double custom

---

PILOTS FOR THE HARBOUR OF LEITH

EVERY pilot to be licenced by the Lord Provost and Magistrates of Edinburgh, under penalty of 5l. Sterling, and to have his name and number painted on his boat

Table of Pilotage

		£	s	d.
For a vessel drawing 7 feet water and under, per foot		0	0	10
Do	8 feet,	0	1	0
Do.	9 feet,	0	1	1
Do	10 feet,	0	1	2
Do	11 feet,	0	1	3
Do	12 feet,	0	1	[illegible]
Do.	13 feet,	0	1	6
And for each 24 hours attendance on board the ships.—To the master pilots,		0	2	0
To each of the boatmen,		0	1	0

Every vessel from foreign ports to pay 1s 6d to the shoremaster, and 1s. for hoisting the flag

Every vessel of 40 tons and upwards, to pay for each coasting voyage 1s 6d to the shoremaster, and 1s for hoisting the flag, and putting up the light.

BIRTHAGE

	£	s	d
EVERY passage boat, each time coming in,	0	0	2
Do. loaded with goods	0	1	0
British vessels, from 10 to 25 tons, each coasting voyage,	0	1	0
Vessels of same burthen from foreign ports,	0	2	6
From 25 to 50 tons, each coasting voyage,	0	1	6
Do from foreign ports,	0	4	0
Do. of 50 tons, for coasting voyage,	0	2	6
Do. from foreign ports,	0	5	0
Do. of 70 tons and upwards,	0	5	0
Do. loaded with coal under 20 dale,	0	0	3
From 20 to 40 dales,	0	0	6
From 40 to 50 dales,	0	0	9
Above 50 dales,	0	1	0
Foreign vessels of whatever burthen,	0	5	0
Vessels with coals, for London or other ports, and unloading any part of their cargoes, to take in other goods,	0	2	6

PORTERS

	£	s	d	f
FOR carrying every cart of coals, not exceeding 12 hundred weight, to a fourth storey, and all above,	0	0	3	0
To a third story,	0	0	2	2
To every lower storey, or to a cellar,	0	0	2	0
For every other burthen of any kind, from any place within the city to another,	0	0	1	0
For every burthen of wine or other liquor, packing and unpacking,	0	0	2	0
For every burthen of furniture,	0	0	2	0
For every lift of furniture carried on poles,	0	0	6	0

No porter to de il in buying, felling, or retailing coals, under penalty of 5l Sterling and ever rendered incapable Porters obliged to weigh coals for the inhabitants, and be intitled to one penny per cart, and no more

By act of council of the 13th of April 1791 The porters of Leith are particularly regulated, and no porter fhall demand more than the rates therein fpecified, and fhall have a copy of the faid regulations, to fhew his employer it demanded, under Penalty of 10s for each tranfgreffion, and forfeiting his hire.|

IMPOST ON ALL FOREIGN WINE,

Brought within the liberties, and privileges of the city Edinburgh

	£	s	d
FOR each dozen of choppin bottles of foreign wine whatever,	0	1	3
Each hogfhead of French wine,	1	5	0
Each ton of do	5	0	0
Each pint of all other foreign wine	5	0	0 4-12ths
Each half hogfhead or quarter butt of do		0	10
Each hogfhead, or half butt of do	2	1	8
Each pipe butt or half ton of do	4	3	4
Each ton of do	8	6	8
Each Scots pint, of foreign fpirits or aqua vitae,	0	0	2
Each English gallon of do and proportionably for any quantity under 30 gallons each gallon	0	0	4
For 30 gallons, and upwards, each gallon,	0	0	3
Each dozen of do in choppin bottles	0	1	0
Each dozen of choppin bottles of mum, foreign ale, beer or porter,	0	0	6
For each hogfhead of do.	0	10	0

All Sterling money

DRIVERS OF COALS, AND PORTERS

TO prevent fraud by the drivers of coals abſtracting them on the road, and ſelling the remainder at the weight taken in at the coal hill

There are ſeven ſetts of weights provided and ſtationed at the different ſtands of porters within the city, and are in charge of the boxmaſter of the porters, who is anſwerable to the city for the ſame, and that one porter at each ſtand ſhall have the care of the triangle and weights, and be at all times ready to weigh coals for the inhabitants for the uſual fee, who is alſo to wear a *yellow badge*, marked with the words—Public Weights; and in failure of the above regulations, the boxmaſter is liable in a penalty not exceeding Twenty Shillings Sterling, and the porter refuſing to weigh coals to be deprived of his badge

Firſt Station of the weights and triangles,—at the Weigh-houſe of *Edinburgh*
Second Station—the Croſs
Third Station—Bailie Fife's Cloſe
Fourth Station—Head of the Canongate.
Fifth Station—Head of the Meal market, Cowgate
Sixth Station—Regiſter Office
Seventh Station—St. Andrew's Church, New Town.

Drivers of coals, to produce (if demanded) a ticket of the weight of his coals, ſigned by the Grieve of the coal hill, and if found deficient in weight, the coals to be forfeited to the uſe of the Charity Work houſe, and if more than a quarter of an hundred, the driver to pay the expence of weighing, and double the ordinary fee

No cart loaded with coals to ſtand for ſale, in the ſtreets of the city, or Canongate, upon pain of ſeizure of the coals

Coal carters to range their carts on the South Back of the Canongate, and in the Lawn Market, and no where elſe in the city.

REGULATIONS FOR KEEPING THE STREETS CLEAN

1 No water, ashes, or other nuisance, be thrown from the windows, doors, or stairs, nor carpets shaked from the windows.

2 All nusances to be laid out before seven o'clock in the morning from 1st March to 1st September, and before eight the other half of the year. Carpets to be shaked or dusted before eight throughout the year

3 Nusances on no pretence to be laid out on a Sunday

4 The possessor of each house to sweep and preserve from nusances, the common stair immediately below such house, at least twice a week, and a storey or lodging being void, the possessor next above is bound as aforesaid

5 No chaff to be emptied in the streets Chaff beds to be emptied by the scavengers

6 No ashes to be riddled in the streets, upon forfeiture of the riddles

7 No spouts for conveying water or nusances from houses shall be used under penalty of Ten Shillings, besides expence of process, and demolishing the spout

8 All dung, bark or timber, laid upon the street shall be taken away within three hours after laid out under penalty of Ten Shillings, and confiscation of the property, and if continued in the street for one night, the person from whose possession it was brought to be liable in a further penalty of Ten Shillings

9. No obstructions of any kind to be left upon the streets, or avenues to the city, on penalty of Ten Shillings.

10. Masons not to hew or drop stones upon the street without permission in writing, and all rubbish, or earth, to be carried off, the same day as laid out, under penalty of Ten Shillings

11. The word Nusance to comprehend dung, filth, herbs, greens, roots, ashes, dust, straw, chaff, bark, rubbish and water And the word Street to comprehend all streets, wynds closses, courts, squares, vennels, and areas, within the city and liberties.

12. For treſpaſſes againſt the foregoing regulations, where no particular penalty is annexed, the penalty for the firſt offence is Two Shillings, for the ſecond, Five Shillings, and for the third, Ten Shillings, beſides twenty-four hours confinement in the City guard or Tolbooth.

Further Regulations.

All perſons poſſeſſing ſhops, vaults, and cellars, under the foot pavement, or poſſeſſing houſes and ſhops where there is no vaults or cellars, in the royalty, ſhall ſweep and clean the plain ſtones and foot pavement before their reſpective poſſeſſions, once every day, before nine o'clook (Sundays excepted) upon pain of forfeiting Two Shillings and Sixpence.

WATER-PIPES

EVERY water-pipe or ciſtern which ſhall be found running waſte, ſhall be entirely cut off, and every water-pipe to which there ſhall not be affixed a proper ball, cock, and ciſtern, ſhall alſo be cut off

---

ERRATA.

P 71 For 5s Duty on Stills where Molaſſes is uſed for making Wines, read 5l

P. 91. S for Saturday, and S. for Sunday, to be left out

CONTENTS.

THE END

CPSIA information can be obtained
at www.ICGtesting.com
Printed in the USA
BVHW04*1133050918
526586BV00014B/166/P

9 781379 519317